A

New

Dawn

By

Jennifer Pickton

Copyright © 2012 by Jennifer Pickton

All rights reserved. No part of his book may be reproduced by any mechanical, photographic, or electronic process, or in the form of a phonographic recording; nor may it be stored in a retrieval system, transmitted, or otherwise be copied for public or private use – other than for "fair use" as brief quotations embodied in articles and reviews without prior written permission of the publisher.

The author of this book does not dispense medical advice or prescribe the use of any technique as a form of treatment for physical or medical problems without the advice of a physician, either directly or indirectly. The intent of the author is only to offer information of a general nature to help you in your quest for emotional and spiritual well-being.

In the event you use any of the information in this book for yourself, which is your constitutional right, the author and the publisher assume no responsibility for your actions.

Pictures from Serif Image Collections and Click Art and are royalty free

    Copyright year 2012 © 2012

    Copyright Notice: by Jennifer Pickton.
    All Rights Reserved.

    The above information forms this copyright notice © by Jennifer Pickton.

    ISBN 13   978-1-291-25750-2

Author

Healer & Medium

Development Teacher

Platform Demonstrator

Jennifer Pickton

Other Books Published:

Books in the Spiritually Inspired Series:-
   Call of the Angels
   Cosmic Connections
   Cosmic Reflections
   The Stream of Life
   At Heavens Gate
   Holding the Light
   Walking in the Light
   Twin Pillars of Light

Books in the Inspirational Shamanic Series:-
   Moon Star
   Mountain Hawk
   Black Raven
   White Feather

Books in the Spiritual Verse Series:-
   1. Man's Bewilderment.
   2. Development and Knowledge
   3. Insight and Inspiration
   4. Colours and Messages
   5. Angels and Healing.

Contents

		Page
1.	Unto Thine Own Self be True	11
2.	The Truth will Set you Free	15
3.	Alignments	19
4.	Healing, Health and Reconstruction	23
5.	Freedom to Higher Knowledge	27
6.	Self Development	31
7.	The Child Within	35
8.	The Shamans Role	39
9.	Freedom to Unite	43
10.	Simplicity	50
11.	Fearful Emotions	55
12.	Young Creative Talent	59
13.	Connecting the Two Worlds Together	63
14.	Yuletide	67
15.	Christmas Tidings	71
16.	Preparing for a New Year	75
17.	Awareness	79
18.	Who are we?	82
19.	Alana	87
20.	Haniel	91
21.	Haniel Speaks again	95
22.	Spiritual Gatherings	99

Contents

		Page
23.	Jeremiah – Old Prophet	103
24.	Nazarene	107
25.	Guides and Contacts	111
26.	Angel Star Healing	119
27.	A New Dawn	123
28.	Britannia's Influence	127
29.	Healers of all Souls	131
30.	Healing specialists	135
31.	The Creative Force	139
32.	Meditation and Prayer	143
33.	The Spiritual Surgeon	149
34.	Many Feathers	153
35.	Newly Arrived	155
36.	The Awakened Mind	159
37.	Forthcoming Changes	163
38.	Your Guardian Angel	167
39.	The Present	171
40.	The Light of the Soul	175
41.	The Future Times	179
42.	Be who you really are	183
43	Love is in the Air	185
44	Changing your Note	189

Introduction

This book is reflective of personal transformation in as much as the theme is of 'being true to yourself' always, and through the transformative process of the present Age of a New Dawn, the individual self becomes True unto itself, as itself realises its true state of being. This allows the true spirit within to emerge, and the true self becomes the lightbeing of a soul, now shinning brightly in realisation, understanding and knowing.

The author did not realise at the start of this book that her personal life would be affected to reflect the major changes taking place, so that transformation could take place, personally, actually and thoroughly. The clearing out process of all negativity is sometimes painful and upsetting, but if the realisation is made of the purpose and reason for such experiences, then the self can open to receive the new energies of life giving properties. The self can embrace the changes as positive indications of incoming new and wonderful aspects of circumstances and experiences, commensurate with the new vibrations of fulfilment, wholeness and confidence. The new state of awareness brings the glory of all that is indicative of God's blessing, beauty and bounty.

The start of a new era in life is always open ended and full of excitement and expectation. All that is positively possible is welcomed into the New Dawn of the New Age. Only the best and brightest is sought, for anything less will not vibrate with the harmony and illumination brought on the rays of love and light.

The Lightworkers have arrived to do their work and enlighten the masses in spiritual understanding and celestial knowledge. We must not forget that science plays its part, as many aspects of spiritual understanding that were previously misunderstood, will be explained and confirmed in this New Dawning. That which was predicted by mystics will be verified as true and correct. Co-operation and joyful living will become the aspirations of the best, so everyone will want to be apart of the New Dawn of co-operative living.

                Love conquers All, as All is Love.

Chapter 1

Unto Thine Own Self Be True

A new life upon the earth planet arrives with an open consciousness, so the eyes and ears and other senses begin to register the new world of dense vibrations, which requires the physical senses to attune themselves for reception. A new born child is innocent, for its mind has yet to absorb the earthy environment, and the physical self needs to become grounded, by attaching the energetic self to the earth mother, as well as to its human mother, who has given physical life form to that child. As the growth to adulthood takes place, the life journey presents many opportunities, and it is the parents or other near relatives and friends, who are responsible for planting ideas for growing aspirations. In time these may conflict with the knowing sensitivity of the very one, who needs to make major life choices.

How many fathers would like their sons to follow in their footsteps? Some cultures are founded upon the generations upholding a particular trade or profession, as in the Indian cast system. If parents are both Doctors it seems reasonable that their children would also enter into the profession and undertake health related work. It may be fashionable to join the arts or sciences, for so many humans tend to follow the line of least resistance, not realising that their inner needs remain unfulfilled. It may be some years later, when a crisis develops that may highlight the issue for change, and suddenly the active life is turned upside down with a complete change of direction.

There are some souls that know instinctively their life role and may dedicate themselves to teaching or researching, or go exploring the world, forever continuing a search for one thing or another. It comes to everyone, at some point in their living life, when the question is asked 'what am I doing this for'. You may find yourself unhappy with your life because of duty and responsibility weighing heavily upon you, and all of a sudden, your personal desires and aspirations surface, causing disharmony and dissatisfaction. This makes you question why you made the choices that have brought you to this present state of realisation, by instinctual knowing. The answers you now know are only partially complete, for the answers received have given you more questions to investigate. It is a step by step process of progression, when realisation dawns and opens awareness, making you seek further.

The evolution of the consciousness is forever expanding and growing in width and breath, as it absorbs new and wonderful scenic views, physically and pictorially within the mind senses, as realisations dawn and bring answers, like dropping jewels of wisdom, which are so aptly timed and focused. So when knowledge is shown to be true, by being acceptable and accommodating, you feel right with the knowing, as it vibrates in harmony with your own vibratory notation. Even with knowledge that is not quite understood, it is absorbed when harmonious vibrations endorse its validity, so truth becomes known and felt, as it becomes realised in manifested form.

For an adult human to move about in the physical world, the values and the reasoning of intellect must be developed forthwith. With every interaction between humans, the mind and senses must discern the truth from the untruth, for much that is true is coated in the fabric of materiality, which may hide its true nature as a way of protection. There are many truths cloaked in tales and fables of old, which can lead to learning and receipt of subtle insights, being hidden gems of great value.

When aired in the light of day, the blooming of a hidden truth, begins to flower, and suddenly all things are understood and the revelation is spread to many, who are able to attune to a release of a most enlightening broadcast. More and more human beings are becoming self-enlightened, and can live their lives in a most truthful manner, abiding by the Laws of Creation, the Laws of Karma, the Universal Laws governing all in manifested glory and righteousness.

When all is open in truth and humanity as a race is true to their inner calling, then the race of humans will unite readily in divine cohesion of consciousness. Then all minds will come to the same realisation and knowledge of true heritage and being, and the 'I am presence' will emerge, so each may attain the godliness of their own true being, as each reaches their individual apex, and joins with the higher-self of being, intune with all that is and ever will be.

The blending and realisation of the consciousness does not mean the surrender of the individual mind, but brings a greater, expanded realisation of all living things, which live and breath within this universe, and in so doing, knowledge and understanding is laid before you all, as wisdom doors open to all the seekers of God's love and illumination. You freely enter into the sanctuary of living truth, releasing all boundaries and limitations. The living light will be your guide for ever more, and lead you to God's love and presence within your spiritual abode, which in the fullness of time, becomes your new home of consciousness and divine revelations.

May God Bless you all.

Jeremiah – Old Prophet

**Absorbing the Seven Rays
into the Human Light Body.**

Chapter 2

The Truth will set You Free.

What is Truth? It is what you perceive to be reality. This is why many humans differ in their ideology for they see things, feel things, know things from the life around them, and this differs with each individual, as each human is unique. How can a human be unique and seek to share a universal truth which is the same for everyone? This is the paradox of spiritual knowledge, as what seems to be impossible becomes possible. It is the wonder of life itself, for life seemingly comes from nothing, to become something, hence the wonder of God's kingdom and the glory of his creations.

The truth is that creativity comes from the unseen into the seen. From an idea within the mind of God becomes a new concept and is formed and brought by magical and mystical means into physical manifestation. The grandeur of ideas can manifest as beauty in art or design, in construction or formation being natural or manmade. A flower is one of natures beautiful adornments and a statue is a man's way of capturing living history. A landscape painting is a representation in time to capture the image of a beautiful scene. In nature that scene is a living landscape. Nature changes with the seasons and by the hand of Man, depicts fields used for farming, or grazing, or reflects the natural woods, lakes and dales of countryside. Truth may be fluid or static, for when we look at the stars in the night sky, we see them in our flat vision.

When in reality the stars are housed in a holographic space where the vision can alter according to the angle of viewing. The truth may be a rude awakening for an uneducated mind, like the discovery that the world was round instead of flat, as it was generally thought some time ago. The fact that nature shows us rounds and cycles at every turn, shows how slow we are to grasp the understanding of the essential basic structures of nature, which have been around us all the time. As a child we are taught by teachers who may themselves be limited in such knowledge or ways. This is where the human can engage in self-education, by contacting the spiritual sources, who will offer teachings from the halls of learning. These educational centres reside in the spiritual realms for the minds of many living beings, to access truths of varying kinds.

Subjects differ, from the many cultures and dialogues existing around the known universe. Concepts and ideas are encapsulated in form structures, housed within the etheric storehouses. These are the blueprints ready for manifestation into outer realisation, regardless of the destination or ultimate focus of expression of a blueprint, the principal structural idea is housed and recorded for all to access. The etheric and physical dimensions are intertwined, as within the physical worlds, it is the etheric matter which interpenetrates the spaces between the parts of manifested matter, and transfers essential particles, being unseen light aspects of vital ingredients, to make up the animated physical form structure.

That which passes through the etheric substance to feed the physical cells and tissues, is the substance which provides life giving essence to the animated form, and is the source through which the divine light of love manifests into material adornment. Three etheric planes send forth their vibrations to become the four manifested streams of physical formation being mineral, vegetable, animal and human forms. Within the human form can be seen the seven energy nodes or centres, rising from the base of the spine to the crown center at the top of the head.

When all is vibrating in perfect accord, the human structural form shines brightly in harmony and balance, and with all systems working perfectly, the human being experiences full and maximum power flow to all its parts. It mirrors the cosmic universe in miniature, for it is a perfect reflection of the inner dimension, manifesting into outward realisation.

The material form is the fulfilment of the etheric blueprint and exists as an expression of spirit in matter. The truth is laid bare for all to examine and for those who do, is given the insight of a divine revelation. A human being is a universe of systems and planets that revolve and circulate within the physical body frame and flowing energy is transported around this structure to replenish and keep active, the many parts and systems interpenetrating the many sub-parts, which make up the whole form. Within the human is seen a reflection of the great cosmos and so many answers are hereto presented, if the view is directed inwards to the mirror image of the outer reality.

A cyclic nature impinges upon the various parts of outer nature, so does the inner body systems renew and revitalise as old is replace with new. Eventually the structure will cease to function and be replaced with another, often a replica, being a son or daughter to continue the line of evolution. Development and growth is always around to bring greater expansion of the physical and mental processes, so that the humans living in a certain time span, can measure advancements, as events and circumstances as they unfold.

Such are the truths of existence for a human being who assesses his or her life, by the amount of time residing upon the physical planet. Remember your other life, the unseen life of thoughts, and the feeling and sensing the energies of other life forms around you, which you know and can sense, even while you live in a different dimension of life.

This is the true reality that gives your life progression, for you will return time and time again, into and out of the physical dimension you presently inhabit.

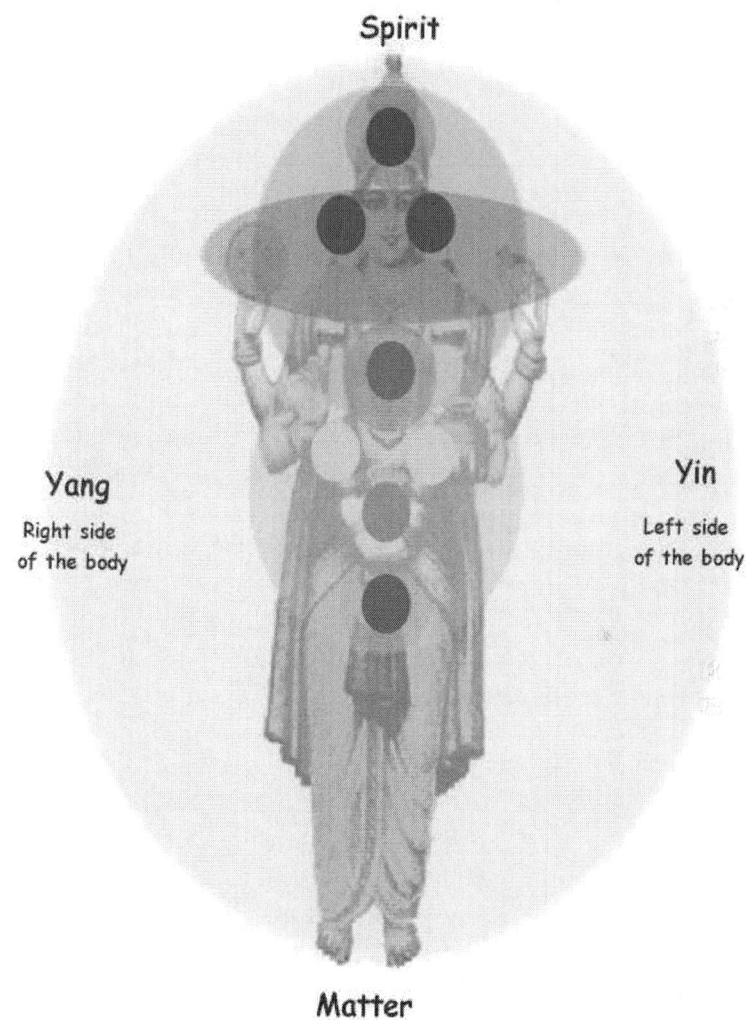

Alignment of Energy Centres 'Chakras'

within the Human Light Body.

Chapter 3

Alignments

You are approaching the time of an alignment of universal planets, so you may see some energy shifts of great proportions. This activity will affect earth life and be felt in the physical events of changes taking place around you. There may be physical phenomenon in the skies and atmosphere, and at high summer, it is customary to experience many sightings of unidentified objects and happenings, and this year will not disappoint. Watch out for unusual configurations in the sky at late eventide, when the sun dips towards the horizon. You may see faces in the clouds, and objects configured amongst the celestial stars and planets. On a clear night, watch out for moving stars for the cosmos is full of activity and your position is great for viewing celestial phenomenon presently taking place.

The Cosmic Lords draw near to humanity at this time, to reassure and strengthen the resolve; to stand straight and true in the understanding of unfolding knowledge and realisation. The true nature of mankind is revealing itself as a cosmic being of great resourcefulness. Already there is a forward group of earth light-workers forming a representation of light and goodness, who are ready to be ambassadors for your planet. They stand to greet the Cosmic personal without adornment of earthly shells as protection. They are the redeemers of your world, for they have learnt to ascend beyond normal thought, and enter into the realms of celestial divinity.

There are four leaders who represent the four elements and a fifth who is a female, to represent the birth and emergence of the fifth element of ether. She holds the torch flame of golden light which acts as the lantern of light to shine upon the universal realms. 'Amoura' is the love of life in emergence, for she holds the hearts of many in her being and presence.

She is indeed an angel upon earth, for her light shines most brilliantly and her passage around your globe is taken with diligence, so all nations may receive her lighted love and realise that within each human being, the same capacity for love and life resides, ready to express itself in realisation and actuality. The present times are indeed exciting, for the changes taking place within and without physical expression, are superseding all expectations. From hidden sources there comes divine light.

From within darkness, light shines as if it were an oasis. The beacons shine forth from your world and your planet becomes a beacon in itself. Little does the average human realise his present status. It is perhaps good that most humans are not average and by necessity have to use their minds in ways not formally taught. It is through the senses and super senses, that the understanding is relayed, and it is received not by the rich and famous whose minds are concerned with earthly matters, but by the lowly, the poor, the dedicated, those sensitive, those struggling, those who are ordinary but unordinary, and all others who feel, sense and know. They are the for-runners of the revealing wave of humanities unfoldment.

The time arrives for many when they must acknowledge themselves as God's servants and know that the work they carryout, is for humanity's greater good and the future happiness of the race. The creative media of images and pictographs are bringing together ideology, which only yesteryear was sanctioned as unacceptable. Present minds can discern fiction from fantasy, but can minds discern truth hidden in fantasy but left out of fiction?

Your world may seem upside-down at times and difficult to understand in logical terms, but the turmoil is around you to shake old notions from mindsets, and to allow new concepts to become seeded and grow. Each generation believes it is wiser than it forbearers, and so it should be, for open minds can absorbs so much.

Discernment in all things is a wise undertaking, so adopt this measure if you can, and you will not go far wrong. Learn to use logic with personal discernment and feelings, to become a light-worker that knows what God's kingdom needs, without ever having to ask or elicit others. So become instinctual by knowing, for you know the truth, that you are connected to divine understanding. You are apart of God's understanding as you live in his being of full consciousness.

Know that to seek service in God's ministry is a calling worth undertaking, so do not be afraid you are not worthy, or ever think that you are not good enough or able enough, for God takes all who show willing; he sees in the human heart, what others do not, or cannot see. Be open and honest in your relationship to the Great Spirit and allow light to flow to you, to show you the way forward. Follow the light in truth and firmness, for as your belief strengthens, your Will Power lessens in resistance, and you begin to blend with the love flow of divine essence, which greets you most welcomingly.

Know then, that the Angel of the Lord has been sent to you, as a messenger and guide. He will lead you surely upon the path of light and illumination. Following in loves wake, you will surely align in righteousness, to realise all things beautiful and true, and so be able to act as a true light-worker for your God and fellow humans.

Four Cosmic Lords in Unison.

Healing Hands in Alignment

Chapter 4

Healing, Health & Reconstruction

Today we are privileged to hear a lecture by an emanate doctor, who once was an earth dweller. The subject is healing, health and reconstruction of physical body parts, as it applies to the physical world of earth. An Angel expands understanding.

Doctors discourse: *This must seem strange to light beings who do not need such services, but it is a subject that is most interesting, as the physical body of a human is so closely connected to its etheric counterpart, that one is affected by the other, as the processes of each are intertwined. The more robust an etheric body can be, the stronger the physical counterpart will manifest. Equally if the physical body sustains injury or suffers disease, the etheric body will show weakness to affected parts but it will maintain its formal structure, as the manifested blueprint of its origin, so keeping an etheric wholeness to vitalise the body double.*

When healing is given, the healing flows into the etheric light body, where reconstructive attention brings fortification to those areas of the physical body, which are unhealthy sites or missing structural parts, for where parts are missing, the etheric counterpart still exists, and in the mind and senses, feeling can occur to verify this as true. Many of the healings that take place in the physical world are initiated this side of life, and may not be detected, as they occur within the regime of natural occurrences and self-regeneration, brought about by the self healing mechanisms within a human framework.

Often the patients own internal being, activates the healing energies, like downloading a computer programme to fix the problem. I am one of a team of doctors all working for improving the healing services to humans and contribute to the evolving remedies and processes which make up programmes of remedial therapies. The present changes in consciousness is bringing major enhancements to receptive minds, willing to engage and accept new ideas and thinking. It is difficult to produce physical phenomenon within acceptable explanations of present scientific understanding.

Many answers can be explained using etheric understanding of energy formats, but how do you explain regenerative bone tissue as a scientific occurrence when scientists will not accept anything unseen? This is the debate being held by the doctors. How to explain the unexplainable? We give the Angels this conundrum, while we doctors have the task of making things happen in the physical world.

Lord Lister had a great following due to his use of antiseptics at an earthly time of un-acceptance. This did not stop him from following his knowing and it eventually led to widespread uses of his methods. This premise applies equally to other known medics and medical pioneers, as does the principal, which can be attributed to other disciplines in many history times. The consensus of thought is to allow humans to come to their acceptance naturally, by helpful discovery, at a time of need. Often earthly events are used to introduce a new method or idea amongst the human population. A new component within the blood can be useful to inspire a discovery for all sorts of things, as it can be carried around the body to become affective at any site showing disharmony. Such are the wonders of modern times, when diverse means are employed to bring sense to the insensible.

When returning to the outside of the temple where this discourse was held, my Angel companion and I could see pathways leading inland to other buildings some short distance away. As we left the temple, there were other humans drinking a golden liquid, which I was told helps new light bodies to attune, and absorb needed particles from within the surroundings. Angels don't need to do this as they float here and there at will. It is only the new human light-bodyform which requires spiritual fortification, whilst it is in its acclimatisation period.

My companion Angel relays much information to me, and offers to accompany me back across the bay of white sand from whence I came. My Angel Guide felt he could answer further questions arising from what had been relayed at the lecture. Here in spirit there is no pressure to absorb and understand information, it is just that opportunities are offered all the time, and it is a personal choice whether to accept help or not. Help of any kind is healing in action.

My Angel Companion explains:- *A new light-form of a departed human, may need a little time to get used to its new environment. The mind and the light-form-body may take different times, to attune into the harmonising vibrations of the spiritual living dimension. Such are the steps of reconstructing life in another realm. Some humans who arrive with great pain and suffering are hospitalised in a sleep condition, so their minds can come to terms with what has happened to them, and once realisation occurs, the pain and suffering quickly disappears, for the light body carries no physical pain. It is the mind which retains past thoughts and conditions, and requires freeing from such burdens. A colour wash system is employed to revitalise the light-body and clear former earthly debris. Lying on a crystal bed and being transported to the sea of tranquillity is a welcomed experience, often repeated by those who feel in need of refreshment or need to feel closer to God's essence, which all can do automatically, when harmonising with the divine essences emanating from source.*

We who are of the Angelic fraternity are always connected to God's essence and need only to raise our thoughts to the higher vibrations, to receive a wave of brilliant light, which brings power to our forms and provides direction to our work purpose. All Angels have specific work to do, as with any administration, the wheels of endeavour bring harmony of action and smooth progress to those who come in need of healing their minds and souls. Angels work willingly and lovingly in God's service, as each has been created for service to the Lord, and in fulfilling our work, we are blessed by God and the Higher Angels who are also our Guides and Teachers.

My work is to help human souls to understand their new living environment, which by offering so much, can sometimes confuse a newcomer. Here in this spirit realm of the upper astral belt, the opportunities are plentiful to attend learning events of lectures and demonstrations. This expands the mindset and may present an individual soul with new avenues it may wish to follow. Some human souls spend little time here before deciding to return to earth once more, as they may feel that they have unfinished business and can best fulfil their remit back on earth. Others are glad they are returned to their spiritual existence and decide to work here, to help those they know back on earth, with matters that promote the greater knowledge of health, healing and reconstruction within the physical world. Working with the great minds of yesteryear can be extremely fulfilling and beneficial when original thoughts arise. Putting them into action by magical and mystical means are skills to learn if not already attained.

All work of healing involves bringing harmony to the body, mind and spirit, so that reconstruction of health can proceed forward. In following the original blueprint for an individual human being, who aligns in perfect accord with the source of all things, the soul within will shine true and bright, be vital and energetic, healthy and athletic. The being will be clean of mind and body, so can glow with life's light as an example to others.

Chapter 5

Freedom to Higher Knowledge

I am Samoa, a Lord of Minoa an area near to Egypt which in my time was the largest populated country of importance and significance. The land was fertile in places where the river waters had saturated the soil, and left the mineral wealth to thrive in the cultivation of crops, for this land was blessed with sun, and the growing of produce was widespread and plentiful. Trade was busy with neighbouring peoples, as the land beside the Nile provides a food basket for the population who live in the more arid hinterland. Inland there is desert, which is fascinating and eerie in its attraction. It is a place where you may meet your God without adornment. The night skies were a pleasure to watch, as from this area, the skies cosmic dance can be seen as a play, unfolding for the viewer, who engages their senses on a starry night.

My time in this place was spent as a merchant, as I traded metals, medicines, pottery and cloth in exchange for food, leather and raw cotton. In my native land, the women were expert craft people and could weave and make lace and fashion material with all kinds of artistry. They could take raw material and turn it into something precious and appealing. Items were produced for either personal or general use. The markets were always full of spices, and dried fruits, all smelling pungent and compelling to the senses, that became overloaded by the many perfumes of the delicious delicacies. In Egypt, the elite housed the knowledge of ancients, and it was to these temples and priests, that I became attracted.

The known sciences were discussed by the best engineers and architects around, which were employed to create grand structures and monuments. The land was unforgiving, as the deserts were always trying to encroach upon the land held by men of means; those who would control the elements in their daily life, and worship Ra the Sun God who was the Grand Provider and life Giver. We ate fish grilled over an open fire and cooked vegetables of corn, potatoes, roots and beans. We drank a whitish liquid that looked like watered milk, but was more potent as fermentation had taken place, and this was like a hock mixture. Corn was used to make bread and stone ground bread was seeded which was very wholesome and filling. Chickens were rather scrawny looking, but they did lay eggs. Most farmers kept chickens and pigs, as they would eat all the scraps. Rice was beginning to be grown near the rivers edge where irrigation was plentiful. Our many olive and nut trees provided a pleasurable array of delicacies. I loved figs and oranges.

Egyptian land holds strong energies. Where the pyramids are located, was an original star-gate portal to celestial and heavenly places. A great being once descended from the heavens into Egypt to bring the peoples advance knowledge. This encouraged many humans to learn and their development widened to envelop centres of great knowledge, where people from all over the known world, could congregate to exchange products and views. A trader's life was a rewarding one, as you met many different people from different cultures and learned so much in the process of interchange, between those of different races and cultures. The best that could be derived from each culture was considered to be the height of contribution to those elite rulers, who would formulate policy for the masses. Only the more advanced and educated men could understand the significances, and so it was, that the simple and easiest route adopted, was to feed the peasant farmers with sufficient knowledge only, to provide for their needs and welfare. Greater knowledge remained in the hands of the Elite Elders who were the custodians of inner or higher knowledge.

This has been the state of affairs for centuries until now. It is NOW, that humans are awakening to this heritage knowledge, of being a cosmic being. It is NOW that the full truth of cosmic awareness can be unveiled, so that the human race may understand and free themselves from the fear burden of centuries, which has acted as a control banner of oppression. No country has escaped this experience. Each human can now make the connections to the higher vibrations of life. You will see a growing need to amalgamate in groups, to discuss and learn more. These groups mirror the gatherings in my time upon the earth planet, when I attended the temple lectures and sat in groups to discuss the future education and evolution of mankind.

The time of NOW is a unique time, as it represents a time for all seed races to amalgamate and deliberate their knowledge and views. As the higher vibrations become absorbed by the planet, the human population will become energised to speak and be heard. Freedom from control, Freedom from oppression, Freedom from fear, Freedom to express, means humans can think for themselves and do not have to take the ideas of their rulers, without first considering the merits themselves. A society of Freedom and Equality, heralds in a New Age of Living. Elders and Governors will look to the general populace for the best ways to rule and serve their people.

General people will govern through elected representatives, who will have to answer to the ones they serve. Values and worth will reverse themselves so that the ones who rule become the greatest of servers and holders of responsibilities. The power of the people will never be so great, and never will people be so aware of the collective responsibility they carry, within the community they live. If events do not go according to plan, then action is required by the people's representatives to alter services, so that the smooth running of societies may proceed.

It is a time of great change, but changes for good purposes and a bright future. Liberation applies to all levels of being, so be wise in your choices of how to use your freedom, for this opportunity may never present itself again.

Mystical Knowledge

Chapter 6

Self Development

Self development should be for everyone, and particularly for those who have experienced an expansiveness of their mind and senses, to find they are more aware than ever, of unseen forces which impact upon them and their surroundings. Life is full of incidences that no one can explain. The more we know about ourselves and our environment, the more questions that seem to arise. Answers are everywhere if we have eyes to see, and the sensitivity to perceive. With our minds we can free ourselves from fear and follow the lighted path to enlightenment and realisation. When the door of understanding opens, we see before us, the light of reason and knowing, flowing straight to us. We become a lighted person, a light-worker if we choose to relay our findings, and understandings, to one another.

We each as individuals have a responsibility for our actions, our own behaviour and our own thoughts. If we aim for the highest and best at all times, and we think before we act, then satisfaction will surely be ours, for all the efforts expended. We may sit back and watch the new found joy and happiness unfold, in those we have touched. We may see the pleasure in the eyes of others, who will shake hands with us in appreciation for all that we are able to give them. All that is given unselfishly will be reciprocated in the fullness of time. It is the Law of Balance which shows us reciprocated actions, for all that is given is returned, like for like, or promoted to flow on to other recipients, allowing new energies to fill the vacated spaces, and renew the balance by filling a void more appropriately, to vibrate anew.

Actions follow thoughts which are energy surges of positive intentions. Once a line of action has begun, then a chain of events may well occur. One incident influences another in a long line of eventful movements, until the overall energy flow weakens to a reduced level, which results in actions ceasing, because of the lack of on-going strength or power. An individual needs constant energy input to fuel the animation of the physical form, and to fuel the mental processes which drive a person to think and act.

The physical body is fuelled by material food, but the mind and senses can only be fed by energy stimulation of ideas and vibrational notions. These flow through the airways to affect the energy body, which is the auric emanation of the physical form. This energy body needs food as much as the physical body, so draws upon the etheric dimension, which is the unseen world of energy formations for all sustenance. The etheric dimension holds within its world, the blueprints or structural plans, for physical forms, that manifest upon the earth world. It does not matter whether it is a mountain, plant or human being, the blueprints arise from this dimension, so it is wise to get to know the source from which all our being derives its life energy, since it is to this dimension that we should notify, should we require more energy inputs, for the continuing growth and maintenance of the material body and mind.

The mind is not the brain. The mind is an etheric vortex of energy being a mind unit, like a computer processing unit. The brain is the physical housing linked to the mind, as its mechanical processor connects to the other parts of the physical frame, which requires animation and co-ordination to function normally. There are electrical and chemical exchanges, which transport messages and instructions to the bodyform, for its continual movement and action. Many wonder where ideas come from. From the brain? or from the mind?

The brain is but a large sponge of cellular mass, saturated and stimulated by nerves and blood vessels, which supply the nutriments for the receptor sites, ready to receive images and dialogue from mind stimuli. This produces the physical registering of ideas and notions you know as sight pictures and heard words, sounds or music. The resonations received to the brain are translated by the physical senses as the lines of communication are activated to the sensory organs. The knowing does not have a physical organ and comes from the non-physical mind within the etheric vehicle of the bodies energy form. It is this etheric body or energy form that interpenetrates the physical form and fills the empty spaces between tissues, organs and individual cells. It is because of this association of the two aspects of mans body structure, that the mind can become active and activated from stimuli flowing from both the physical body and etheric body, as they unite in a compatible fit.

The etheric body form is slightly larger than the material body, so the contour or outline can be seen by some humans as extending beyond the outside skin, by about two or three inches. The human form is like a fruit which has a fleshy body housing a hard stone or inner core, which holds its key-parts for growth and regeneration. Like the fruit which uses its fleshy covering for nourishment in the early growing times, so too does the human use its etheric parts as a media for transporting nourishment arriving from outside of itself. The fruit that is planted in the soil will absorb nutriments from the earth to enable growth to begin and flourish and when stems and leaves have grown, the plant can then receive more nourishment from the air, sun and rain, to complete its life cycle. Human feet stand upon the ground. The etheric part sinks into the ground and absorbs the Earth's nourishment in energetic terms, and likewise the skin around the body absorbs energy from the airways surrounding the physical frame.

From the top of the head the etheric covering can absorb cosmic energy, transmitted and flowing from sun sources which influence the mind. The sun brings the light and warmth to your planet and within the sunrays are contained a multitude of colour rays, which are vibrational forces to stir action into physical life forms throughout the globe. Once brought to life the evolvement begins with daily maintenance from the sun, moon and stars, as well as from the earth mother, who supplies the kingdoms of nature, for all human earthly needs. Such has been the physical growth of humankind.

From the time of self awareness, the human mind has searched for its origins, trying to make sense of the present world with varying success and understanding. Mankind has grown in spiritual stature as he has absorbed the cosmic influences and responded by demonstrating the skills and beauty of eras, showing architectural elegance, painting and sculptures supreme, music and singing of elevated scores. In recent times the engineering and technical expertise has shown prominence with many human minds expanding in the sciences and cultural arts, each opposing and expanding, only to realise that they come together in the grandeur of excellence. The stage of present times is one of self-development and understanding. As the human psyche has developed, so has the capacity of the human heart. Together the mind and heart will work to put into action those deeds of help and healing, for everyone less fortunate than the best and most privileged. All men are equal in the sight of GOD and so should it be upon earth. Uniting in fellowship is the key to success and prosperity, for no man is an island, and no one individual can or should carry the weight of many upon their shoulders. Each is responsible for the self and once you are comfortable, you may extend your responsibilities to those who are connected to you the strongest. These include relations and friends. Those who are missionaries and crusaders have strength to venture further and heed the cries of others unrelated, and offer to them all that is within their power to give, by way of service, help and healing.

Chapter 7

The Child Within

Every adult soul that becomes an earth being, remembers their childhood as a time of enchantment, wonder and mystery, for each day was new with more interesting things to see, hear and learn. The rising sun, a storm of snow, the howling winds and the calm of seas, are witnessed for the first time as wonders to behold. An elusive rainbow brings magical elements within a framework of fairytales, to heighten the curiosity of a child whose inquisitiveness knows no bounds.

Look within, and find the child who is free from fear and imposed boundaries. Seek out the hidden youngster, who searches for mystery and magic in all things. Make friends with your inner child self, so you may gain the hidden pleasures of adult self – regeneration, which grows into new appreciation and delight, upon finding something of interest. Remember, that children also have an unruly side to their natures, and woe-be-tide, the adult who resurrects the childish tantrums of uncontrolled emotional outbursts, when the word NO was the signal to sulk and be disruptive. The agonies of non-acceptance are hard lessons to learn, so do not make the mistake that all childish attributes are favourable. It is the creative element and newness of approach, which every child exhibits in their upward growth pattern, which enables the learning and growing to develop to a well balanced human adult.

Acknowledge the good and greatness that was within your youthful growing time, as these benefit your adulthood, as you can look back and view times of simplicity and silliness, softness and pure heartedness. It is the pureness and simple values that children accept wholeheartedly, that makes the brightness of character, for the full grown man or woman to exhibit. Seeing the funny side of things always uplifts the spirits, and to be able to laugh at oneself, is indeed a gift, for it shows that you do not take life so seriously, and can adapt more easily to changing circumstances. In a lifetime of living, the pains of growing, flowering and dying are felt and witness all around in nature and in human communities. When adverse events touch your own life, it is a difficult time of adjustment. You may be strongly affected by a deceased relative and find life harder to bear as a consequence. In time the burden becomes easier as life moves on, and newness replaces that which has since passed. It is the way of things, and part of the cycle of life that revolves with regularity, to bring the emotions to surface anew, with every turn of the wheel of life experience.

You continue to learn at every stage of growing until the day you die and return to your spirit region. Even then you do not stop learning, as your mind and knowing is freed from earthly confines, and more scope is offered to you for your spiritual expansion. The universe is expanding so why shouldn't you? If the human is a cosmos in miniature, then the same rules that governs the universe, also govern mankind. The present times are one of lightness and most expansiveness for all humans residing upon the earth, who willingly embrace the cosmic vibrations into their physical being. It is the light essence of the spiritual dimension which is the cosmic heart energy, uniting and unifying the hearts of all living humans, so they may recognise that they are part of a universal being, whose heartbeat is felt alongside your own. You are a human being, one of God's creations, moulded in his likeness.

Many are aligning themselves with the Mother Earth Being who recognises her beating heart, being in tempo with the universal source. The Sun being of the galaxy brings life support and warmth to earth, and allows the human, through his sight and senses, to physically witness the oneness of all physical creation. Look around you and see the cycles of birth, development, flowering and recycling, so new forms may grow and take centre stage, for all to see. It is the wonders of God's beauty and eternal flowering, which brings so much pleasure to waiting hearts. A child is always open to the sun, moon and stars, for they want to know more and use their imaginations to contact the power sources of the universe. Children bring the imaginative dreams into the physical awareness of earth life, to enrich and bring pleasure to those not so able in their awareness or physical form being.

It is to the free spirit of a child that the spark of divinity is given, to shine brightly and clearly around those who have attracted darkness to them. Illness and diseasements are sure signs of darker elements that are often tempered into neutrality by the presence of a child's spirit. It is a child's spirit that can see the spirit of others, as clearly as physical sight shows the colours of earth and the splendours of nature. Take time to learn to reconnect to your inner child, for you might learn a thing or to, about yourself, about things you were unaware of.

Unblocking forgotten memories can have beneficial effects, for all housekeeping of the inner self, can bring unexpected discoveries and rewards. It is like taking the varnish off an old table, layer by layer, to reveal some exquisite inlay of mother of pearl. To find a diamond is rare, but who knows what can be unearthed. Perhaps the one who is willing to experience a discovery may find a diamond of sorts, as the explanations reveal new gems in an otherwise mundane package. Your inner child once found, can become your best friend, for he/she will never be very far away from you.

You may want to integrate your child into your adult being, so you can become as one, and that is just fine. Together you can shine brightly for others to realise their inner selves, and like you, come to a time of integration. Know that wholeness is to be encouraged, for all aspects of self should be acknowledged, just as all times of life should be recognised, as a journey or process, towards the flowering of your true self, that spirit within, which makes the individual who it is.

Fairy Tales

Chapter 8

The Shamans Role.

The true shaman is called into service through life's difficult pathways and he or she is tested for endurance by circumstances arising in the personal life, to be overcome by learning the lessons provided by experience. The physical body is subjected to trials and tribulations which impinge upon the mind, to find the total acceptance to this understanding and way of life and living. The shaman is the connection between the energies of earth and all creatures, and the greater energies of spirit and creativity.

A Shaman learns to blend his or her energies with the elements of water, fire, earth and air, and wields these energies with positive force and intent, to bring about desired aims to manifest in the physical world as helpful healing remedies, or processes to bring self-understanding to those who make enquires of the shaman for personal enlightenment. The shaman can enter into his altered world of seeing and feeling, by journeying within the etheric mind band. He can find answers for himself and others, to fulfil quests to reveal life's unfoldment, both personal and collective. He can connect to ancestors who act as guides and mentors for education and insight. The ancestors are a wonderful connection reached by engaging these powerful energies, for it is through the ancestral linage that the source energies flow, and much understanding is forthcoming when a good connection is established.

The ancestors have experience of earthly and heavenly spheres, and can advise in ways unimagined, as they hold so much wisdom and knowledge. One mind is sometimes overwhelmed and responses from other individuals are such, that they also become overwhelmed. To the uninitiated the shaman can seem strange, for they demonstrate a mixture of old ways with old and modern understanding. Simplicity is revealed in the general understanding of natural occurrences which abound in every age and in every time, and with the use of the drum and drum beat to summon spirit vibrations, revelations of health, healing and future happenings are acquired.

The use of stones and bones for divination purposes can sometimes seem peculiar when marks and signs are arranged for interpretation. All nations have their equivalent of a shaman and they can be called by other names and include witches and witchdoctors, healers and herbalists. The shaman works by journeying into the spirit world to find missing soul parts and brings to an inflicted helpless soul upon the earth, the balancing parts which make up the whole being of physical expression, being the human body, mind and spirit. An individual may be suffering from hurt or disease when the Shaman is called to chase away the unhelpful spirit influences causing upsets.

In the world of energies there are many energy spirits without form and as such they cannot be seen only recognised by feelings and sensing. A shaman will identify such energies as spirit sources bringing various qualities and values with them, to determine their own existence within the etheric realms. The shaman may use songs or chants to enter into the spirit world, where he may be assisted by animal guides and helpers to facilitate a healing. The vibrations of resonance allows the shamans spirit to enter into the body of the one who is afflicted, and who needs unhealthy parts restored to harmony, balance and wholeness. Many shamans are integral in the society in which they live.

They may be male or female and be ordinary workers during the daily life activities, using their gifts and talents when called upon for special occasions such as high days, cyclic events, seasonal apexes, and personal requests. Female shamans may be versed in the healing arts and double as a midwife, to bring new life into the physical earth world. Others may have extensive knowledge of local plant life, herbs and crystals, which bring added benefits to a community, and be incorporated in ceremonial activities associated with moon cycles and seasonal changes. At marriages and funerals the Shaman is in attendance to centre the focuses of unity and release. With marriages, two joined souls unite as one, to become a unified force within the material life, and shape future events for both to enjoy and appreciate.

At a funeral the shaman deals with releasing spirit forces to unseen realms and releasing the grief of those left behind who are suffering emotional upheaval. Ancestors are called to attend and help the distressed spirits and to clear a pathway for all lighted thoughts, to enable the departed soul to find its allotted space and spirit home. Crossing the great divide from physical existence to the spirit world can be easy or difficult. The departed one, needs freeing from the earthly confines, so burning bodies comes as a ceremony to purify the pathway of release, so no vehicle of denseness remains to cling to a disturbed or distressed soul.

For the living, the Shaman can be a blessing at times of great upheaval for the Shaman can look at the life path, and see what best steps can be taken, when tackling the present circumstances, which may seem distressing and disturbing. The Shaman may be called upon to give direction to a group or tribe so that the future undertaking of the collective peoples may press forward in confidence. This is when the ancestors have great input, as those who have gone before can provide good advice to present humans and their living life.

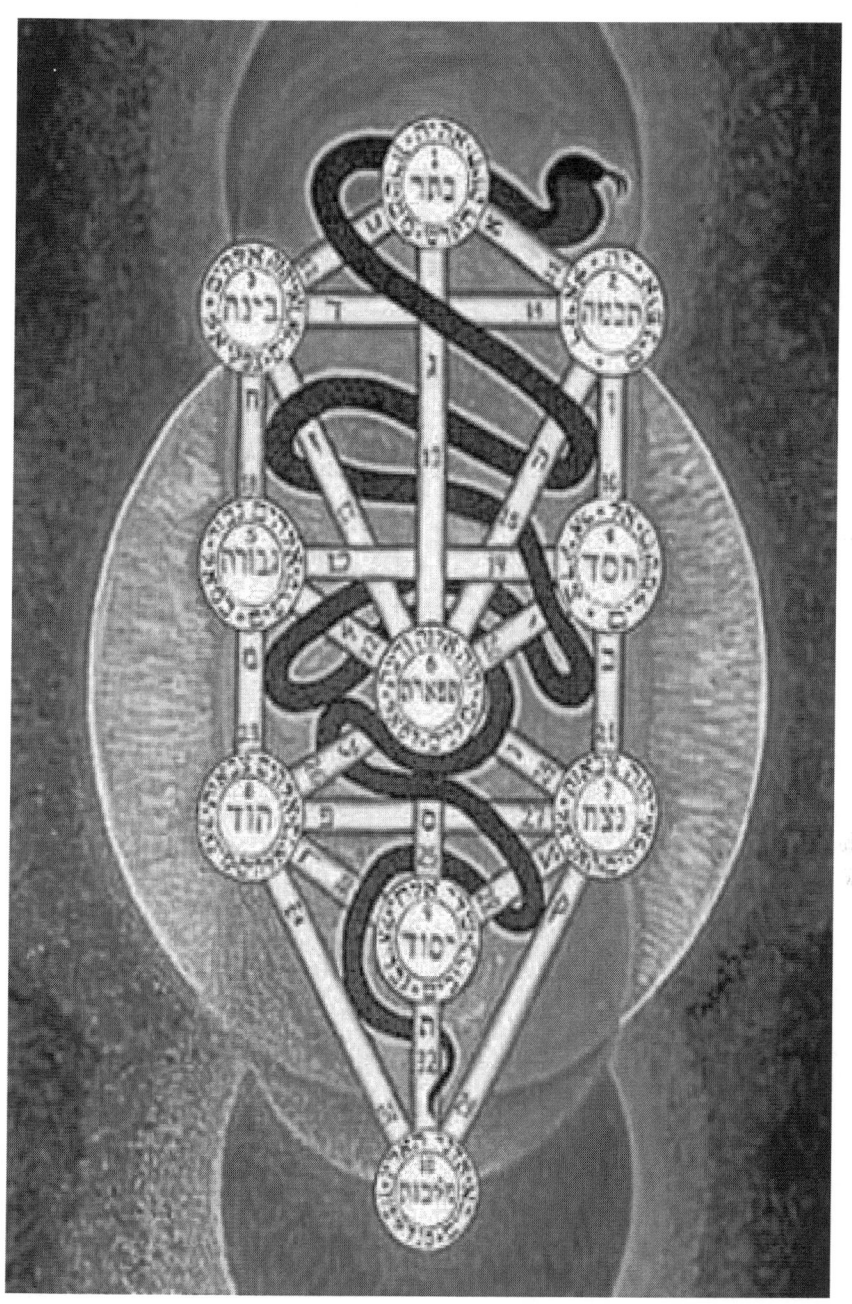

The Tree of Life

Chapter 9

Freedom to Unite

During the adventures of a life experience, there arrives a time of becoming stuck in a situation, where it is practically impossible to extradite yourself from your position, without the help of someone, or something else, offering you a helping hand. It is always embarrassing and frustrating when you have tried all sorts of ways to overcome a difficulty, and still find yourself stuck within its ridged confines, as you remain unmoveable as before. The more you seem to struggle the worst your situation becomes, and the larger your difficulty grows. It is not until you realise you have little choice but to ask for assistance, that you actually do elicit help.

The waiting for help or any sign of relief, can feel a long time, especially when help comes as other willing hands to lend their energies to you. You may be given added power and ability to literally fly over the hurdle that is blocking your way. It may be that the process of extraditing you from your situation or circumstance, will take some time, but from the moment you receive recognised help and assistance, the worry and stress levels fall considerably. You can laugh at your mistakes or laugh at the situation you have found yourself in, as you can now look back and see the wrong turning you took, with clear eyes and understanding. Often fear and fright, generate distress that lives with you for ages after a traumatic experience.

There is nothing like compounded fear to manifest as physical signs of distress within a human body, as this is a response to it being put under stressful conditions. All symptoms of physical distress are the reactions to some kind of stress factor, which has been felt by the emotions, being known incidences or even unknown incidences, where the sub-conscious has recognised a former underlying stress condition, and has reacted by compounding it. The mind sometimes has a mind of its own. We think we are in control of ourselves but we are not always aware of our uncontrolled reactions, which respond to situations as automatic reflexes and unconditional responses.

As an individual matures and enters into senior years the mind becomes wiser, but the sensitivity of the emotions remains just as high, as when you were ignorant and un-knowledgeable of life's ways. It seems that life has opposite ways, for as children, fear is unknown until experience and events has taught otherwise. The elderly citizen of earth has lived through turbulent years and some have weathered better than others. Some humans have immersed themselves in the living life and have not freed themselves from the trappings of materiality or the confines of social dogma within which they live. It is surprising sometimes to see senior individuals still holding views and opinions that they gained when they were youngsters. They live restrictive lives of their own making, because they do not bother to change with the tide of present living conditions.

There are others however, who embrace all that life throws at them, good and bad they say 'bring it on'. They welcome life in all its guises because it is the roller coaster of life that brings thrills and sadness, and yet they would not have it otherwise, because of the benefits the high points of glory brings when life is at its best. These are the young at heart people, who remain young to material life at every turn.

Only their human bodies age as years pass, and many hold back the pressures of time by their youthful approach, to life's many pleasures and unfolding interests. It is those humans who embrace the youthful attributes to learn all things and never give up on learning whatever the subject matter, who remain eternal students. They like new things to try out, to see if they are improvements on existing standards. Many mature humans embark on a project of learning by taking up some interest they were not able to pursue, during their younger days. Whether this is painting, handy crafts, dance, music, history, film or media pursuits, the interest alone brings an added dimension to their lives. Where this is lacking, there shows a lack of sparkle and a loss of life vitality. Depression seeps into the living life and those who are uninterested in life's many attractions, soon decline in health and die. Death comes to each one at a designated time, pre-programmed within the Genes and DNA of the structural body.

The human can opt for a life fulfilled or a life of sameness leaving the spirit unfulfilled and unsatisfied. There is an approach and an attitude to adopt for living, so that the very best and most, can be gained from living the physical life fully. Children live each moment and do not worry about tomorrow. Adults can minimise their stress and fears by adopting a more optimistic view. Soon you will find that positive views and notions attract other positive energies to you, and good things come your way. It is self projecting and self-profiting. In your modern vernacular it's a win, win situation. Think then on the ways to improve your general life, aim to examine your motives for the things you do and say, and your general approach to others and situations. By changing to more optimistic viewpoints you will find a general improvement in your life events, and suddenly you will find you no longer harbour fears of any kind. When universal laws are understood by the majority of the human population, then will overall improvement emerge. Like attracts like – a simple truth to test.

Contemplation on Life

The more you think good thoughts, the more good things come your way. If you desire something specific, try imagining it coming your way. Do not become fixated on the idea itself, just think clearly and positively to allow the energies to work on your behalf. If it is possible and the energies become aligned, you will receive your thoughts desire in the fullness of time. Remember that motive plays its part, so be wise to make requests that are positive and pleasing, as any negative or wrong motivational thoughts will fail to please.

Learn the universal way to be happy and free. Try loosing desire in the becoming of your realised self. When you stand with no fears, you simply are yourself. Others treat you fairly and do not judge you, as you do not judge them. Do not offer any criticism unless you are asked to do so. It is a way of keeping your own counsel. Those who discriminate with their thoughts, words and sayings, are considered wise and considerate.

It is easy to smile and bring pleasure to someone who may not be feeling well. It costs nothing to say hello and smile to your neighbour. Try being nice to everyone you meet in one day and see how you feel at the end of that day. Look out for those who smile at you, and notice those who are willing to help out if the need arises. It becomes infectious being nice and friendly, and it is surprising how many people respond to you. Those who would never voluntary stray from their set pathway, are inclined to deviate to sample the sunshine of life. When they feel safe and secure that the road they are sampling holds no dangers, they quickly leave the old road for a new sunshine pathway. The knower who lives the earth live of NOW, can bring so much pleasure in simple ways. So much light can be generated from simple and pleasing actions and thoughts. There is pleasure in giving and sharing, and there is pleasure in receiving and passing the same to others.

There is pleasure in being amongst like-minded people who share your ideology of being simply loving and giving of nature. It is not a lot to ask in this modern materialistic world, so start by being such a person, who brings light and pleasure into another person's world. You will receive blessing for doing good deeds, as good things will be done unto you. Everything will be good in your earthly garden, so you will feel rich and whole. You will become rich and whole. Whole of body, mind and spirit. Rich in health, well-being and life position. Free from the burdens that others seem to suffer from in their earth living.

You have found a way of overcoming the difficulties of life by a simple and true manner. Start by marketing this find. Start my promoting this find. Start by educating this find. Start by becoming the epitome of this find. Many will look up to you, want to be like you, and wonder how you have become such a light-being in so short a time.

God works in mysterious ways, his wonders to behold!

Look no further than your heart, to feel if this doctrine runs true. If you cannot find fault with it, adopt it for your own, and you will never again be without light in your life.

Never again will you be without love in your life.
Never again will you be without companionship.
Never again will you feel confined, as freedom will be yours.

Set your mind and spirit free in the physical world and allow your spirit self to fly into the heavens. Bring a little bit of heaven back to the physical world, and show your findings as you smile and light up the lives of other human beings. Know as you do so, you are carrying out God's teaching of loving and helping your fellow human beings, and are demonstrating what the Brotherhood of Man means in this life of materiality, when simple ways can refocus thoughts and emotions, to bind all souls into a united Brotherhood.

Sound Healing

Music for the ears is given,
When perfume to the senses is driven
To join with light of visual sight
Become notes of colour, vibrant and bright.

The beams of power exceedingly large
Convey the sounds to move and barge
Upon the senses in one crescendo
A volley to reach an archipelago

The spirit sores with such delight
When music reaches endless heights
For once the movement has begun to pace
Then all can follow, and make haste.

Stir up the emotions, stir up the vibes,
Gather together, and become a tribe,
So you can sound with one great voice
Rightful difference is a personal choice.

Your note is heard, it sounds most strong,
To force the righteousness from wrong,
So all is cleared, to make the pure
In heart, in mind, the bodies cure.

For once you are, that streamlined form
No earthly worry can bring you harm
For you are armed with knowledge wise
So sound your note to take the prize.

Healing Light

Chapter 10

Simplicity

All physical manifestation starts with simple expressions of energy formats, as the expression of spirit is always that of simple, pure and clear love. In the manifestation of physical matter whether it be star formations or a human being, the physical manifestation of form begins with the simple division of one cell into two, or the joining of two into one, then splits into three or more. From the simple to the more complex is the gradual progress of evolution, as the forms grow and become a greater construction of complex patterns, being the evolution or development from the original simple blueprint of its origins.

Spirit is always expressed simply, because it is contained in the essence of love. Love is the element which is the most misunderstood, for the human has relegated love as an emotion and does not regard it as an essential element or power within all living things, which it is. The word LOVE represents - **L**ight **O**f **V**ital **E**nergy or **L**ight **O**f **V**ibrational **E**ssence. The Light and Love are interchangeable energies, for where love exists, there is light of being or understanding. Where love resides, the being glows with light and can be viewed by those who posses the clear seeing faculty. Other's who inhabit the material plane of existence see it in the beauty of creativity, as displayed in nature or in the arts of man's expressive capabilities. The human race holds within itself this love or light of divine manifestation which makes a human, a God in the becoming. Only those who recognised this element within themselves, can openly manifest the light of their being, and do so by their actions, thoughts and deeds.

Many times it is not the conscious aspect of the mind which recognises the essential light of the soul within, it is the unconscious aspect which is capable of connecting to the higher aspects of being and life. When a human consciously does make that connection, it brings into being a realisable proposition of manifesting light within the material world of expression, in many more ways that hitherto it has been able to do. Light and love is infectious, as once expressed within human populations who find it to be beneficial, it spreads out in a most contagious way. This is good, for the more that humans can recognise the spark of light existing within, and know it is a divine spark from the great creator; they can then emit such vibrations to others, in a chain of love and lighted ways.

The more the streams of illumination of love and light are spread out into your world, the easier it will be for all people to come together, and join as brothers in the great band of human brotherhood. When essential truths of divine understanding are greatly appreciated by the majority of human souls, then it will be the time for the race of humans, to collectively stand united, and be as a true God of the universe. ....

The wise ones of the cosmos look on in anticipation of human achievements, as the human race is beginning to absorb the finer vibrations sent to lift each soul being. More humans than ever are looking to the star people and outwardly for answers to their troubles, affecting worldwide relationships and economic survival. Fear is everywhere and is self perpetuated. Wise earth dwellers detach themselves from the worries and concerns of earthly life, and focus their attention on the higher aspects of being. This way the light of reason shines upon troubled waters, to bring solutions to the front of attention seekers, and thereby enlightening common folk who are receptive and open hearted. The way forward is to see simple truths in all circumstances, and find soul liberation which sets free the spirit, which can overcome all that is.

The spirit is a part of all that is, and when adversities arise, it is up to the mind-self to rise up and see the simple solutions that may fix the problem at hand. It is the simple solution which is the most effective, and it is usually the giving of love that rights relationships and situations, to bring a turnaround of fortunes to the positive, so energy flows upward and outward to fuel life and life events, enabling progress to proceed. Beginnings start with simplicity before arriving at the complex, so when the complex becomes too great and starts to crumble, it requires a simple solution to reduce the structural pattern to a manageable size. By simple means the solution is rendered to end a complex dilemma, and change it to a more simple arrangement, which harmonises all aspects most effectively. Normality reigns once again and progress can also proceed once more.

Evolution is full of starts and stops, with simple and more complex designs and patterns, all trying to find a balance with the powers and energies prevailing. Actions carry great momentum of power that fans out, far and wide. The effects of changed energy can have different effects according to the levels of power, affecting different structural densities. The barrier existing between the physical and etheric worlds is now quite thin, and in places has become nonexistent. This is why many humans residing in the NOW time, can visible see with the naked eye, things such as lights and movement, which belong to the etheric world and overlay upon the physical.

Places retain energy from long ago and can replay a scene if the right energy is activated, and so visions of ghosts are seen as an echo of what has been. At other times spirit loved ones visit their relatives and may not realise that they can be seen and perceived, by their kin upon the material world. Humanity is waking up and seeing with their clear seeing eyes, more than just the physicality's of material existence, but also the underlying energy formats, that substantiate the material existence and manifestation of life as you know it.

The simple explanation is that the world of matter and non-matter are but vibratory existences, and as such can be seen and lived in, if you as a being vibrate at a similar rate. It is the development of the human being into a cosmic manifestation, which will enable manifested existence on all levels of being, regardless of prime placement within the universe. Humans are already doing this, but are not aware of this fact, so many are having to relearn this truth revelation, in order to operate as a cosmic being in the true sense. Such are the future revelations and abilities.

Man's Emergence from the Life Force

Chapter 11

Fearful Emotions

The spread of fearful emotions is expanding amongst the nations as the outcomes of financial repercussions from recent events are postulated in the media, to fuel fear and outrage. It requires calm and clear thinking to solve problems, so no amount of emotional outpouring, will solve the difficulties that loom ahead. It is the human way to find out things from experience, and a wise man will recognise failure and turn to something else more feasible to tryout, when replacing a seemingly unsolvable situation. People power can make or break a nation when the common man gains his say. Those who live under democratic governments can see that their governing electorate no longer represent or uphold common thinking. Representatives are allowing the political power of an elected position, to take over as the prime target of focus.

The common man has a voice to be heard, for he does not want to be beholden to anyone, and would willing give up much for the right to choose, and the right to be free from government meddling in his personal life. Most adults of average education and understanding can manage their own affairs, if given the right moral and ethical inputs, as guidelines and boundaries. The current generation have been misled by governments and media expectations, and even school education has geared the young thinker into believing he can accomplish his dreams, when the real world of material existence, remains a conflict of who can overcome another. This situation occurs irrespective of whether the conflict arises in the expressions of physical and material existence, or the emotional and psychological areas of a person's makeup.

The corporate media is as corrupt as the governmental media, in any democratic regime. The organisations have become too large for the personal touch, and as a consequence the lines of communication become distorted and sometimes forgotten altogether. More simple structures can be seen in the co-operative organisations, where folk are equal members and contributors. Their work may be different from each other but their contribution to the whole is equated by the hours and effort given over to the whole. Each takes responsibility for their own patch of concern, and glories at the outcomes they can reach and the quality that is produced. Pride takes equal status to remuneration, so that the soul can glory in the efforts and rewards, of personal creativity and giving.

Wealth is measured in the satisfaction achieved and the feelings of wholeness felt. Being a part of something good and actively pleasant is rewarding. Work should be fun, enjoyable and easily rendered. Rotation of skills and jobs give greater interest to boring and mundane occupations. Incentives and competitions are great fun whatever the cause or environment. If a man wants to change his trade because he thinks he has a skill or wants to further his interest, then existing avenues should open doors for him, to try out his undiscovered talents. These may be training schools for occupations such as shopkeepers, community carers, gardeners and therapists. Some may want to create as artists, jewellers, actors and comedians. All these occupations contribute something to the value of life, irrespective of whether it may be necessary for living or for pleasure purposes. One uplifts the physical body; the other uplifts the mind and emotions. 'Which one is better' can only be answered, by an individual at the time of their personal need. Value can be generated by personal input or quality of substance. It is often un-measurable material that acquires value by way of mass demand, for something that is quite scarce. Once the item becomes more accessible it looses its high value and becomes more attainable by the many.

New discoveries are such and are examples before mass production becomes available. Where the value is based upon a finite quantity the costs remain high, until views are altered to focus upon something else, when demand falls to lower levels. When certain items cannot be distributed any more at high levels, they have to conform to commonality, if distribution is to take place. Commonality is referred to as within the ability or capability of the common man to achieve or acquire. If only the elite are able to hold items of seemingly high value or worth, then resentment will arise to divide men from each other. If however by personal ability, achievements can be rewarded, a scheme open to all is offered, and no one can complain of those who meet the challenges put forward as all rewards are attained by personal effort.

Fear is an emotion that will prevent the individual from trying to further their aspirations. If you are told by someone, you are not good enough or that you do no have any talents, you will believe a mistruth, for every human has some talent or gift that they can offer to society. Every human has a personal aspect of themselves, which covers up a talent or gift. Someone gifted with words may be a great storyteller. They could write a play or book. Others may have singing voices, or be able to act. They may be good organisers, good recorders, care for other less fortunate who may have medial issues or educational problems.

Many occupations cater for personal qualities to be present for if they are not, you receive an automation service and not a human service. The emotion within human beings makes them the feeling and sensing being that they are. H.U means 'High Unit' reflecting the complex structure of creative form which contains the power of receptivity from both positive and negative streams. This means that the human brain has receptive capabilities to accept energy formats from the material and cosmic sources. The brain of a human is divided into left and right hemispheres in line with the duality of physical existence.

The two parts are connected by a central channel with can become united to enable working cohesively, giving the human consciousness access to two worlds. When both hemispheres are balanced and can work in unison, there cannot be any fear based emotions, for the one side counters the other to being enlightened and this light's up all parts of the human framework. This brings healing also, as the cosmic consciousness is part of the whole, and when a human can access the universal mind, all is understood and made clear. Oneness is wholeness, completeness with the source energies.

No Fear

Chapter 12

Young Creative Talent

It gives me great pleasure to communicate with you again and relay to you, our latest news. Many of my students are graduating as they have grown and developed with absorbed knowledge, and have taken in the God light that is so beneficial to personal progress and expansion. It is like graduation day when students have reached a required level of attainment and can now move onto a higher grade elsewhere, or go into the living world to take up work suitable for their talents and abilities. Many of my students are joining with the Great Masters to help with energy refinements, needed for the ascension period, when humans need a helping hand to adjust to changing vibrations.

My students have graduated to aiding the mechanics and engineers of universal calibre and status, assisting the inter-connective-ness between dimensional spheres. Lines of light you may say, and this is true, for the end result will be to connect lines of light together, so flows of life properties, can be transmitted to enable minds and souls, to travel inter-dimensionally in ways newly opened up. The portholes of universal alignments are providing the energy structures through which the lines of light can pass. It is like a new door opening to emit light from another place into a new room of darkened energy. Light illuminates and transcends darkness, so all is surfaced, and can be viewed in light and understanding. New approaches and ways of comprehension are opening up within the human psyche, and this enables the minds of many souls, to access places they have never been before.

Even spirit beings have not been everywhere, so this phenomenon is as exciting for us, as it is for those humans, who can transcend the barriers of earthly existence, and travel into the spiritual dimensions. Learning and experiencing is for everyone irrespective of locality and residence. God is everywhere and within all things, so where light travels, our supreme being is felt and registered. The universal heartbeat is God's heartbeat and when we can hear or witness this sound or vibration, we know that this Great Spirit guides and loves us, for he is showing us his kingdoms and giving us opportunities to carry his wisdom and truths to all parts of existence.

The universe is a large place, never ending you may say. If there is an end, it could be at the outer edge where unknown voids exist. This is a part of Gods energy that sleeps, for all is tranquil and at peace. It is like a blanket enfolding the known universe, keeping it contained, safe and secure. It is where the pure energy resides and where the souls of evolvement that have reached the highest levels of development, decide to dwell when they give up all form and individual consciousness, to join with the God forever and eternally. They become one with the body of the source, pure energy of divine essence in complete wholeness.

It is from the source energies that life, as you know it, comes into being, both physical and non-physical, and to where all life will eventually return when the Great Cycles of existence have run their course. All that is and ever has been will implode as pure energy, to reside together once again, until the stirring of God's will, evokes new outpourings of energy, that will start the creative processes once more. The life of universes are vast, for within a creative mix, there is much activity of life coming and going, revolving and evolving to new complex forms, and becoming stabilised or falling apart. Over periods of activity many forms stabilised and life forms may reside upon a planet, if conditions are conducive for that life expression.

Many planets in the present universe have life forms, but not many can say they are actually physical forms. Many forms are those supported by the planets substance and may be gases, fiery or highly energised or lowly energised, with varying levels of intelligence. The Great Cosmic Lords wield their powerful dictates to determine the avenues of life programs, for they see the promise contained within, and fashion energy to align with conceived thoughts. They carry out the will of God for their own energy is strongly close to the divine source, and their attunement is totally focussed. Only divine thoughts are received and actioned, for the will of God affects all close divine beings, who cannot help but serve the Great Spirit, whose knowing is their knowing, for they are the outsourcing of his being, his universal action beings, who oversee his creations.

These Great beings, the Universal Lords, are the custodians of God's power and stand as sentinels in space/time/existence for the presentation of creative substances, the alignment of energies and colour, and the containment of gases and denser materials in motion and flow. They are like a father who sets off a firework display, for around them creation shows as newness and renewals. Many colours, lights and sparks ensue, and they light up areas of seeming darkness that effectively energise voids of space, and produce a most splendid sight of colourful interchange.

My students learn from such high voltage beings, so they can help in works of creation and progress in ways they feel they are most suited and attracted to. Your work with students gathers apace, as they are showing leaps of development and progress, personally and collectively. Keep up the teaching and gain satisfaction when facilitating new channels for spirit. I am always close by so when you feel you require some advise call upon me and I will influence you to enable the knowledge of spirit to flow freely forward.

Alana – Light Being.

New Species

Chapter 13

Connecting the Two Worlds Together.

Students who progress to the standard of ability, which allows them to relay messages from spirit in an open forum, realise that the interpretation of feelings, ideas and senses, need a quick processing response, to enable the lines of communications to be acknowledged, and verified as fast as possible. This is to facilitate spirit nearness of a loved one to become identified, and in so doing, students are able to bring the necessary information within the energy formats, which carry recognising factual features and memories, to an identified recipient.

Many relatives of those residing in spirit, who are presently earth dwellers, seek communication with their loved ones, just as the ancients sought communication with their ancestors. Some humans do not believe in communications between the worlds of earth and spirit, and are sometimes surprised when it is they who are picked to receive a spirit communication from a relative or dear friend. Once the shock of realising that life and living continues regardless of earth dwelling time, the psyche opens to new possibilities, and a new view on life itself is presented. Spirit communications can be the healing needed, for many humans suffer grief at the loss of a loved one, and to know that they are indeed thriving in the spirit world, is a much appreciated snippet of knowledge, which usually uplifts and heals many current hurts and also those of longstanding.

The road to becoming a clear and competent channel for spirit is not always an easy route, for human minds are self-deceiving. Societies that foster logic, dominion and physical science, often subdue anything that cannot be explained within physical existence and understanding. Proof is always sought for any phenomenon, which will substantiate a premise. It is to be applauded that current students of mediumship are seeking specific ways of making sure, factual and evidential information finds its way into the communications between worlds. We also congratulate you on all the efforts to bring the emotional content of a loved one forward, to meet the needs of the physical relative. The chosen recipient knows without words that their loved one is nearby, just by feeling and registering the energy notation, which they still remember and revere. Mannerisms and quirks of character are all aspects of a human's makeup, which can be relayed in communications, to colour and strengthen the verifying process.

Proof is subjective and objective, as a recipient's memory may be sluggish and slow to recognise information, which will be presented. Stated facts may be clear later on, when the memory throws up revealing data which has been stored deep within the mind. Often this becomes good evidence, as it has had to be investigated and verified by consulting others, for it to be accepted. Many humans pray for all sorts of things which are personal to them. They reveal hidden aspirations and yearnings to the unseen world, when they send their thoughts and requests into the ethers, with the premise that someone out there will answer and act in their best interests. That someone out there is elusive, so elusive that no one can describe the source, yet every human knows there is a source, for everyone who prays beseeches the heavens for a God, to intervene in some manner. The God source is forever being hailed to right wrongs and change disturbances that in effect, human beings have instigated and brought about themselves.

It is the spirit beings representing God's countenance that impinge the influences upon the human psyche, so that a sensitive human can receive guidance, appropriate for their current problems and life circumstances. By recognising and acting upon such influences, the guiding knowledge transforms the living life to a much improved state, whereby the human and his surrounding fellows, are actively encouraged, to act for the betterment of their current conditions and circumstances. This is normal working practice by spirit guides and helpers, which attach themselves to individual humans, whose Guardian Angel or Guide has hailed for assistance.

The guardian guide is the first port of call for any human, when they make a request from the earth realm, and it is advised that the human being, now present upon the earth world, be wise enough to cultivate a channel of communication, with his or her guardian guide. This close connection will benefit the living human in many ways, not only for everyday life activities, but for the communication to other spirits, who can relay knowledge and information from other dimensions, and seek to educate the human race upon their cosmic heritage, from which they have evolved.

This knowledge and revelation is necessary to open the human psyche, to enable individual sensitivity to rise to levels commensurate with spiritual levels, where the two worlds can join and unite in harmonious accord. This will enable the heavenly attributes to become incorporated within the new earth vibration, and in due time and an appropriate period, reveal a heaven upon earth. This plan has been seeded within the race from the beginning, and is now at the point of becoming a material reality. The earth planet is saturated with lighter vibrations coming from celestial sources of stars and galaxies, beyond Stargate limits. Celestial beings in co-operation with Cosmic and Universal Lords are overseeing the Ascension process, whereby the human race and the planet Earth are brought into alignment, with the central source of all being.

The consciousness of humans everywhere is widening and many minds are travelling to pastures new, when they find themselves day dreaming or asleep, in meditation or an altered mind-state. So much is transmitted via the subjective senses of a human that the conscious being has a hard time sorting the real from the unreal. What is often missed, is that the unreal or fantasy in one dimension, is the real and factual in another. Those humans whose minds can reach a higher sphere, can converse with beings that abide there, and can bring back knowledge and experiences from such realms, to enhance the earthly living and grow the knowledge of understanding, thereby connecting two worlds together.

Mystical Lands

Chapter 14

Yuletide

The cosmic portal is now wide open and the new energies entering the earth's atmosphere are flowing forward to dilute the denseness of earth's energy mix, to bring a more fluid and lighter mixture of finer hues. This allows the surface inhabitants to inhale the new vibrations without noticing any great difference, and then the effects will not be noticed until realisation occurs, to those who recognise these subtle energies, as being of universal origins.

The celestial entities are surrounding the earth planet at this time of yuletide, for the flows of energy have to be monitored, and the effects seen and adjusted for, as the programme runs in form, to work out according to the great plan. The Cosmic Lords consult the blueprints of this great task, and like any great programme, it is the forward planners and organisers that take the lead, to show how the flow of events will manifest.

The nature kingdom is working its magic and the elementals are more active today than they have been for some considerable time. The consciousness of the planet is awakening to full awareness, as are the many humans who pretend not to know, but do realise that something is afoot. It is like the expectation a child experiences for Christmas, when he or she becomes caught up in the joyful stream of emotions, given out to be friendly to everyone at this time. We of spirit are taking advantage of this goodwill towards mankind, for the energy lends itself to good works of all kinds.

Humans in power are still human at their core, and it is to the human aspects that the present energy focus is directed. Common sense, common understanding, level headiness, becoming reasonable and showing good judgement are ways to improve the general living conditions of many peoples, wherever they may reside upon your world and in whatever circumstances.

The Yule Time is a period, when the less fortunate are considered, for there are still humans living in poverty who lack even the basic commodities for living and existing. They may be in other countries, but even within your own country, there are humans living below the level of accepted living standards, and this demonstrates how easy it is to revert to basic instincts, when the veneer of human sophistication is removed. Desperate men do desperate things as do desperate women. Survival occurs in all countries to a lesser or greater degree. Governments have systematically tried to address this problem and may charitable institutions exist, as evidence of goodwill and benevolence. Throughout history those men who have been fortunate to become wealthy, have become philanthropists to show consideration for those not so fortunate. Through the efforts of one man, others have benefitted and so the chain of flow continues, as the outpouring of good thoughts, deeds and welfare are distributed.

It is often the case that when a man or woman has lost everything, and has been relegated from high to low, that the experience has changed them for the better. It has made them realise that they had overlooked matters of importance. Surprisingly friends made when at your lowest are true friends, for they ask nothing in return except your presence and friendship. When you are stuck will the trappings of wealth and prestige, there are always those who desire what you have, as they are envious and can become friends with two faces. Greed is a nasty emotion which eats away at goodness and beneficial welfare.

We ask that this time of Yuletide, is used to re-evaluate your own circumstances, so you as one person, can make the necessary resolutions for your New Year. If one person can make changes, then another may can also make changes, and with a strong wave of good intentions, the overall energy for forward willpower, will be positively charged.

If you can manage to realise only ten percent of your original intended programme for change, you will have tipped the balance for positive effect. It takes one little step to start a new journey – one that will take you to Heavens Gate, by travelling along with the stream of life. By travelling with the life flow, you can align your own energies with the prevailing note around you, so you will experience less turmoil and buffeting. A calm ride to experience change, is given to all those who are in-tune with current vibrations, and those humans which can express the exact or near notation from within themselves will truly enjoy the harmonious atmosphere in which to operate.

At times of good will to all men, the atmosphere and relationships between near relatives and friends become congenial, and many humans express words of good fortune. This action acts to energise the prevailing time, so we of spirit send our blessings of goodness, to endorse your sentiments and add sparkle to good wishes for your human families.

Blessing for the New Year of 2012
Aquarian Light Weavers

Changing Times

Chapter 15

Christmas Tidings

The light of God's love shines brightly upon you as the day of Christmas dawns. The Angels sing out praises and blessings to all who would listen to the celestial airwaves, and those who feel with their sensitivity, literally tingle with energetic vibrations, in response to the prevailing sounds and scintillating energy waves, as they circulate around your atmosphere.

The light beings of celestial formation draw close at this time and surround loved ones gathered in groups. Young children are excited and adults are expectant in joyous moods to bring about a harmonious period over the next few days. Good will is paramount in many minds during this Christmas time and what better time than now, to show actions of goodness to others in a willing manner.

Please know that the year of 2012 is a prestigious year of great meaning, for history has it logged as an end and a beginning. It is an end in a sense as the past year ends, and a new year always ushers in new energy formats. It is perhaps more prestigious this year, as the energies are so more potent and the ushering in of new energy is that of transformation, helped and aided by living creatures residing upon the earth's surface. It is every human's goal to contribute to the welfare of another, and add to the culmination of change, to bring about a more equable society and regime which demonstrates stable and secure workings.

This applies to all countries and each may differ in their way to accomplish this goal, but the will of the native peoples can bring about such conditions, if all focus upon the will 'to do good' in every avenue of life. Your human history has shown what you are capable of, and with increasing awareness of true life values, the choices and opportunities lay open before you, to choose wisely and recognise the opportunities of good fortune.

Be forward thinkers, be forward planners, be forward in your actions to lead others in your chosen dreams, and make your dreams a reality to be proud of.

Love cements all together,
Love fortifies and Love mends.
Love forgives and Love builds, by pooling with others who give their love freely to a collective whole.

There is no ideology that fits love, for it is a cohesive element that is found in all good emitions, which gel the elements of goodness. When love and light is found within the darkest of regimes, you know that God's hand is present, and even if all is thought lost, it will not be, because the light of God's hand will win the day. Where a little flame of light is present, it can fire up a whole forest blaze, when given the right circumstances.

It is up to all, to create the conditions for the ignition of all lights hidden and seen, so all God's light can be seen rising, to demonstrate the glory and wonderment of loves attainment. For love will prevail, as love is 'light of vibrational essence' and where life exists, so does the flame of light itself. Know that the source of life is the one flame to which all others are derived.

Therefore the coming times of new energy will release much that has been hidden and savoured, for the right time. This time is the right time to surface all light energies, emotions, aspirations and dreams.

- Hold the Light in front of you at all times, and your pathway will glory in positive unfoldment.

- Defeat all darkness and negativity by turning your eyes and hearts towards lighted endeavours, and always keeping your focus to the light.

- Choose to use positive endeavour in words, actions and thoughts and you will truly realise a golden time for yourselves and others. Your surroundings may be in chaos but you will be vibrating with the present notation of this age, and you will rise above discordance into accordance.

- Notice how you attract goodness towards you, notice how people gravitate towards you, who want to help and aid you in your endeavours.

- Notice and realise that the workings of positive energy bring about congeniality, and applying the love code in your life activities, really does make all the difference to the quality and status of your living existence…

……Jeremiah – Prophet of Old.

Follow the Light Upwards

Chapter 16

Preparing for a New Year

The White Brotherhood assemble for discourse so that you can start this new year with right energy, that will take you full steam ahead in the relaying of information to others. We welcome your contact and channel, through which we can send knowledge and necessary data for humanity. We send our broadcasts to many throughout the earth world, so that our words and messages can be brought to the attention of as many humans as possible. It is difficult for many of your race to equate spiritual living with that of earth living, for your societies and your governments seem slow to react to their peoples cries, and so many humans have to continue with struggling longer than would seem necessary.

Be comforted in knowing that every endeavour from a pure heart and clear consciousness is acting to help some other person, who may be experiencing what you are experiencing, and that is why you feel so strongly about injustices that relate to your own personal living conditions and containment of happiness. You can all benefit from the meditative process which lifts the mind states of human awareness, to levels where the discomforts of earth living are no longer registering. This is because you have raised your vibratory note to a higher level, which is above the turbulence of emotional battering, and you have entered into the calm seas of love and light. This is the true state of being, when your soul is not grounded in dense materiality.

When humans allow their minds to fly free of their physical forms, they can sample the delights of tranquil settings, which bring healing and upliftment to human forms at all levels, being body, mind and feelings. Any harmonising of these three vehicles of expression, bring about a most welcomed state of wholeness, and if this can be achieved on a temporary basis, then it should be known that by extending this state on a more permanent footing, it will bring about a greater balance, which when achieved can generate general good health and wellbeing. The optimising of good health and good living is aided by positive thoughts and regulated living, incorporating physical movements and mind full practices. Setting time aside for mindful practices is part of a regulated living regime, which aids the systems of life housed within the human bodyform. Good sleep and general exercise, moderate food, water and sufficient shelter are prime requisites for anyone. To wake up each day, alert and ready for an eventful day suggests a vibrancy which is sufficient for most general work carried out on normal days. By evening time there is satisfaction earned from accomplishing your tasks and forwarding the plans of your current enterprise.

Many humans do not have the luxury of normal living and can find themselves caught up in troubled times, by the fact of being in a certain place at a certain time. Circumstances not of your own making may enfold you, and you wonder what life is all about. You are an ordinary person, floating in a sea of turbulence and you are fighting to stay afloat. You may not understand the reasons for such turbulence, but you know you have to construct a vessel that will float while others may be sinking all around you. The vessel of your construction is not a physical one, but a spiritual one, for you are asked to construct an energy field of light that will act as a coat of armour and protect you and your family. If you learn to shine your light of truth from within to without, and combine your light vibrations with those who think and understand likewise, you will find you are indeed sidetracked by the outside turbulence, and become an island within the great sea of disquiet.

If others recognise your light and energy you will find they want to join you, and within a short time, your small group will become a larger group and your island will expand more and more. The turbulence around you lessens as your island grows, for you can no longer feel the disquiet energy. Your own generated light energy is now much greater, and overlays upon your surroundings. You cannot be moved by outside turbulence, for you have weathered the greatest buffetings, and now you are strong with love and lighted strength to show that you can live in harmony and peace.

When those who fight become weary of their actions, they too will decide your example is worth trying. When the rhythm of life has overtaken anarchy and shows that peaceful ways are more beneficial to human living, the human spirit will then respond to the lighted energy as distributed by those who have embraced this vibration, and who are now the operating lightworkers of the New Age of Aquarius. In every city, in every country, in every land, the lightworkers will operate independently from governing rulers to show how living conditions and relationships can work when peoples of all cults, beliefs and persuasions join with common aims and aspirations.

When they come together to live, work and play, as a community, the basic aims from each person or small group will find a common denominator within other ideologies, which are also seeking a compatible compromise so everyone can be happy and comfortable with the majority held view and aims. This way of everyone contributing, brings out the best for all to abide to, and can pacify many who would rise up to challenge anything they may disagree with. When elders are honoured for their wisdom instead of being disregarded, then respect and consideration is brought forth and recognised as worthwhile contributions by elder statesmen.

Honour is restored to its rightful place and balance is restored where disquiet once reigned. Love binds human beings together and can bring about some wonderful relationships of greatness. Vision is rewarded by the positive outcomes of putting into practice known beliefs and suppositions, so that when events manifest as predicted, all become believers at the sight of manifested glory.

…………………..Brotherhood of Light.

New Season of Glory

Chapter 17

Awareness

As your awareness opens in purity and faith, like a flower coming into full bloom, the beauty and serenity of the experience is most revealing, as the event represents the fulfilment of endeavour. With a flower, the petals spread out like a satellite receiving dish, ready to absorb the sunlight's powerful energies. This it does and converts the energy absorbing particles into life giving energy substance for the plants upkeep and nourishment. At the centre of a flower there is the central stamen and this area can differ in construction with each species of plant. It is the central operating and transforming unit, which takes the energy substance into the stem for assimilation into food fuel, so that the plant can operate and maintain itself.

The human being is not so very different, in as much that he or she absorbs cosmic vibrations from the sunlight and atmosphere, which is used for the sustenance of the human unit as a whole. The human unit is more complex than a flowering shrub, but similarities of processes do exist. The human individual is a physical and energy unit combined, and as such the energy aura impacts upon the physical kernel and vice versa. When the human consciousness unfolds to full flowering, the energetic self of the human, opens to cosmic and spiritual sources, and like a funnel, directs divine intelligence to itself to feed the soul within.

The physical sun and atmosphere may feed the physical human bodyform, but the full flowering of the human consciousness has an effect upon the energetic auric field, which literally lights up the whole being, and is of a transforming nature to bring about cures and wholeness. This is because the soul has been touched by an awakening torch, which activates inherent properties contained within the human constitution. The flowering of a human being is often likened to a flowering plant as it displays the best and highest attainment of that being. The fact that it is also a most beautiful display and revelation to the individual, and to any spectator, does not do justice to the event, for this happening is the recognition and joining to cosmic sources in full consciousness, whereby the soul, mind and being, becomes knowingly connect to its source creator, and can henceforth abide in the heavenly realms simultaneously to living on the material plane, where the present mind apparatus resides.

Many at this time upon the earth world are aspiring to attain this level of being, as they realise the fact, that the human being is also a cosmic being, with ancestral heritage in both realms. Many human races have possessed this knowledge, and for a long time this understanding has been held in store for the right moments that coincide with the flowering of humanities group consciousness. This is what is beginning to happen in the NOW time. As individual humans reach their zenith of realisation, they open the light portals wider, to allow others to see clearly and become the torch bearers of the New Age. New and old understanding of spiritual truths, are merging together, to become generally understood by the common man.

The Media of written words, image carriers and your light networks, reach all areas of your globe, and enlighten many with images, words, sounds and impressions, to bring greater evolvement to the human mind-set. It has been necessary to allow material advancement to take such a high profile in order to bring spiritual understanding to a new light level.

This brings a working media into being that can activate the right brain functions, so it may display the super sensitivity, now becoming more widely viewed. The senses of the human physical bodyform are crude instruments for receptivity of cosmic reflections, but once fully developed, the step from basic to full operational functioning of the super-senses can be accomplished in general, with good speed, if integrity and good connections are continually maintained. In the developing of the super-senses of Clairvoyance, Clairaudience and Clairsentience, the equivalent energy centre or chakras, are developed further to accommodate the universal elements and energy. It is these non-physical energy vortexes which are located within the auric field and overshadow the main bodily organs, necessary for the physical functioning of a human, which are the prime sources of active receptors for the present human incarnate.

If the vibrational mix is in disharmony the effects will be felt within the physical form, as an upset to the body system, which needs constant attention to keep it functioning in a balanced and optimised manner. This is why regulation of life activities is beneficial to a working human unit, particularly if meditative activities are incorporated into the everyday regime of a working and operative human light being. The meditative practice slows down the physical vibrational activity around an individual, to enable the consciousness to focus on the inner being. By spending a little time housekeeping the inner self and allowing the soul within to grow and shine its light, the life and general living conditions of that human individual will improve greatly by bring the whole being into a well balanced state and alertness.

When the Mind, Body and Soul are suitably aligned and operating in full strength, the energy levels of a human being are supercharged. Vitality is visible seen, clear-seeing is the norm, and there are greater heights to audibility noticed with the increased level of awareness.

Bird song becomes a new sound to appreciate, the wind whistling through trees turns into coherent whispers, and the sound and smell of the sea and rain, are something new to bring about further invigoration as energy is felt clearing and cleaning, retuning and refining as the symphony of sounds create an alternative experience realm, where the energetic being is literally transported to an altered state of realisation. The many mansions of Gods house are truly awe-inspiring, and the majority of humans living have yet to enjoy the full glories of their own world in its many dimensions.

Those who hold an artistic ability or appreciation will become star-struck at the many new experiences opened for humans to appreciate and enjoy. Attempts have been made by your talented musicians to capture some measure of natural phenomenon, as they have perceived beauty within unseen dimensions which they attempt to emulate. The light dances, the celestial sounds, the ascending senses take you into the light worlds, upon the paths of purity and love.

Interacting Chakra Lights

Chapter 18

Who are we?

Many at this time are seeking to understand their heritage and are looking at their physical parentage and ancestral charts in order to trace back in time and history, the personalities and events which have shaped their family and indeed themselves. Many more people are cataloguing images of relatives together formally or socially at happy times, to create a memory album, of past times and events. This is not only for present day family members, but may be used as a time capsule for family yet to be born, so that they may have easy access to know their heritage more quickly, as it has been complied in readiness of their questions and seeking buy family members who were thoughtful enough to prepare such information. With modern technology the images of past and present can be stored in ever increasing quantities and moving pictures can also be easily stored for future viewing.

When inroads have been made to achieve genealogical information, many unknown events and details are revealed. The size and members of a family, the occupations undertaken, and the whereabouts of homes lived in, are details recorded in the periodic census and parish lists of births, deaths and marriages. Many family members are now able to trace their ancestry way back into centuries past, when records within civilised countries were first introduced. Beyond this time it is fortune that bestows information in documented form, such as navy lists, military ranks, pioneers and notable personages who have highlighted their lives in some way, and become known in history recall during action times of note.

Without genealogical information, other sources can produce interesting details. Industry provides information on trade and details of individuals and transactions which have survived. House purchases and tenanted lists are all sources of changing information on people and places and going back further when reading and writing was not universal, the elite always documented major happenings and those who were involved. In civilisations where the written word and records are not so prevalent, the population recalled heritage by word of mouth, and in the stories they relayed to each generation, the knowledge of heritage was remembered. Many of the ethnic races still hold to this way of heritage recording, and it is only in the NOW times, when all human populations have been uncovered, that the heritage of each nations, race, tribe and group, is becoming recognised as a personal culture and is becoming documented for world history.

Many of the ethnic peoples can trace their heritage back far greater than modern man who dwells in civilised countries. Often their culture is connected to their religious understanding and is interwoven within their customs to keep alive their beliefs and core knowledge of how they came into being, from celestial sources, and that is why they continue looking up at the stars for their source of origin. When seeking the same answers from a spiritual perspective the modern activity of regression to investigate past lives, brings great understanding to the present personality and soul residing on earth. Present personal are the sum total of all lives lived, so it is logical to credit regression as an activity which can unblock residue negativity, inherited from past lives and living, but which has seeded itself within the subconscious, to be hidden away so not to be recognised. Some people in today's 'NOW' find they suffer from phobias and fears they cannot explain. No sooner do they undergo regression to explore past lives, then they realise their present life has been made much easier and freer than previously, for they have freed themselves of attachments.

The human mind-set is a fascinating media to explore for no two minds are the same. Where one person uses logic and focus to delve into the hidden depths and deal with issues of mind and emotions, another may be totally illogical and follow one avenue of thought and then another, as their fancy dictates, and yet they too can benefit from a personal housekeeping exercise to relieve baggage and burdens that were not realised or explored before. With a spring cleaning of the psyche to relieve heaviness, most humans will return to being a pure light channel, and the effect is to feel 'reborn'. A flow of light energy ensues, to fill that being with a new purpose and endeavour for their life's work.

More and more humans are experiencing this cleansing of mind and emotions, as they deal with immediate issues and relieve themselves of un –needed and unwanted baggage. The search begins for their spiritual heritage as their personal awareness expands and begins to develop. Sensitivity enhances awareness, and nature and natural experiences all contribute to the widening of awareness and growing sensitivity commensurate with personal growth and development.

Once on the spiritual seeking path, the call of the divine light is forever drawing a seeking soul forward into greater and increased light. Thirst for enlightenment by way of esoteric knowledge is unquenchable, and all that was meaning full in the material sense, begins to be less important and less attractive. Even friends, relations and associates that once pleased, no longer shine as important, so a feeling of isolation can be experienced as the soul lets go of material anchors and begins to move in its own right into the lighted avenues of new interests. Soon that soul will find like minded fellows who are also seeking enlightenment. Together new friends are made and groups formed to further enquiry and enhancement of each others journey towards greater understanding of their spiritual heritage.

Understanding dawns: the human is not just a physical form with a label attached to it, to say who it is. The sensitivity brings insight to the person's auric field, which is the magnetic-electrical power energy circulating all human structures. This is a human's workshop containing his toolkit. From his auric field, a human can sense atmospheres, places, other humans, emotions and desires. Reading the aura is like reading a book, some are more open and enjoyable than others. Some are light hearted and others deep and unfathomable. Such are human temperaments.

Within the human aura is contained all that persons hopes and aspirations. Some will come true and others may be wishful thinking. What has passed and future expectations are also housed within this electro magnetic power field. This is why a good psychic can read an aura and be extremely accurate in the details when telling you all about yourself. Predictions are sometimes made from the aspirations logged within the aura as desire can be great, but not all aspiration are fruitful, so may not come true. This explains one difference between receiving information from 'human energy fields' virus 'spirit energy fields'.

When a sensitive person puts themselves forward to work as a medium, they are taught to differentiate between the different types of energy, so they can determine the source of their information. When engaging the spirit world, who provide information through the faculties of the super-senses, being Clairvoyance, (clear-seeing) Clairaudience, (clear-hearing) Clairsentience, (clear-sensing) and Clair-cognisance, (clear-knowing) the information is known by the energy it comes with, so it determines the source by recognising the note of call. Reading auric energy may seem flat in comparison to the vibrant interchange of a spirit communicator.

Once more the human has realised and become a greater being than his ordinary self, for he is now an operating light-worker for the New Age of enlightenment.

Chapter 19

Alana

My dear it gives me great pleasure to connect to your vibratory note, as the airways open for connectivity. My classes of students like yours have enlarged, and there are many new souls seeking to connect to God's higher power. It is the desire of alignment to higher learning and increasing awareness, that brings the spirit of a human being, into recognition, so that the spirit raises its sights and aspirations to seek new wonders of expression, that will take it to fulfilling the sought satisfaction, which overrides all other current desires.

It is the power of the new energies that are providing the impetus to forward thrust the human race into a new era of personal awareness and group realisation. All spiritual eyes are looking to see the take up and absorption of higher vibrations, as the effects of cosmic energy proceeds. The spiritual hierarchy are excited by the present human response, as many souls are reacting positively to these higher vibrations, by awakening inner connections of concealed knowledge, which have been buried and confined to deep mind vaults.

The heritage knowledge of seeded nations from cosmic sources is beginning to arise, to reach the surface of consciousness, so that old knowledge can be brought into the light of day and be examined in the 'NOW' time. Now is the time for great revelations, so graduating to the higher levels of awareness is easy, once the known knowledge becomes available to the mass of human mindsets.

This will free human spirits from the confines of their self-imposed prisons of materiality, and self-interests. Once it is known that humans are cosmic beings and have a spirit which can live at any vibrational level if rightly attuned to that level, by virtue of their personal and group development, then it becomes the greater understanding which will enable the race of humans, to evolve to the next level of being. This next level when fully realised, will be the light-being or etheric coat, which will resonate and display the inner light, so that a human being can be recognised by other light-beings, who may not have a physical or material form base or structure. Recognising energy levels and energy substances is part of the comprehension of how the universe is constructed, and what constitutes manifestation is the spirit in matter, from however lose or dense particles there may be available for the spirit to use, as its cloak of expression is in that energy realm.

It is exciting to see the release of souls from material bondage, for I see many evolving spirits seeking directions that are keen and newly awakened from sleep conditions. It is like viewing a field of flowers coming into bloom, all at the same time. Once the field was darkly coloured and now it has changed its' colour altogether by displaying and releasing the lighted essence. The souls shine with lighted colour most brilliantly. As you draw near to this manifestation of lighted shine, you cannot help but feel the love and blessings encapsulated in the emitted perfume. It is a most heady experience, bringing upliftment to the soul, expansion and wholeness to the spirit, so you know that God's presence has had its effect, for when his lighted shine is seen, his hand has touched the region, leaving its effect of brilliance everywhere. It must always be remembered that the light within and without is God's purity in expression, and that which emits the light is part of the God structure, for we live and breathe in his being, we are part of his divineness, we are part of God's being and within all souls his essence resides.

Never are we alone for the divine source knows all, and if we need a friend, help or consolation, we may ask the source, for the source provides all things so our needs are met in miraculous ways. By the many servers of spirit, we are assisted at every level, and in every service of personal and group need. We all have a twin soul, a companion, who resides on an upper level. This way everyone is in service to another, in a chain of linkage to the Great Creator. All is held together in continuous lines of light, all scintillating a different tone or note. Hence the Great symphonies from celestial beings that use sound and light to create and renew. Always the winds of universal seas bring sounds and understanding from distant places, so the knowledge can be circulated to the ends of time. Where time ceases to be, then all is known, as all becomes one. There is no past, no present and no future – only 'NOW'. It is a state of being, of expression, of being alive and joining with all that is and realising the 'I am presence".

My students learn fast and many are now assisting the Cosmic Lords in their work around the universe. My present students are keen to understand the human mindset and listen into the human chatter for short periods. It is the human emotions that are always the most difficult to understand, but they can be the most rewarding, when understanding dawns. The human is capable of so much if directed positively and correctly. Beauty is so important to development, and is often forgotten when basic needs are sought. Beauty can be seen in your human nature, and in any culture the artistic natures present aspects of natural beauty by manifesting as items, signs and symbols, depicting the beauty as best it can.

All that is at its best displays as beauty, for beauty can be seen even in the most mundane. The snowflake or ice crystal is most beautiful in its inner structure, and so is a human being when unadorned and unaffected. May the beauty of your present time become apparent to you, so you can recognise the beauty of spirit help, and the knowledge that is brought to you.

Treasure this beauty and pass it around to others who may also benefit from beautiful energy, given in freedom and love, to encourage new beauty to blossom into being. My love is given to lighten your work, so you may shine your light with ease and surety. Shortly you assemble with other light-beings who will show their energy, and you will find you are transported to my home where love and light resides in abundance. We will talk again soon and try out other forms of communication... Adieu.

----- 0 -----

Your new guide is strong and forceful. He is strengthening your clairvoyance and channel of direct communication. He will be more active with you when you meet en-group as the energy will be stronger and you will be within a protected environment that you trust and feel comfortable in. The Nazarene is overseeing this arrangement as your new spirit guide is known to him and will be able to spend more time with you, to become closer still – when the book words flow you know then he is close. Patience and all will work out. Concentrate on earthly things to clear the space, so you will be free in your mind to undertake this close contact. You are doing well with your students and they are enjoying the work. We are pleased with the progress, as you do not know all the aspects of effectiveness your work generates. If you did, you might be surprised.

A Rose of Beauty

Chapter 20

Haniel

I am Haniel, Angel correspondent to humanity. I come to you to greet and make my presence known, as I will be influencing you in your relay of words and speeches. At this time of Ascension it is our purpose to influence as many humans as we can, and by contacting and working through open channels such as you, we can reach many more minds and souls.

This method of contact enables us to put our influence into awareness of meanings, which can be more easily understood, for concepts are not always able to be verbalised in simple ways, or be readily absorb through spoken dialogue. Many minds hear the spiritual callers, but cannot give recognition to the broadcasts, because they do no have the conceptual ability within their minds, to make sense of the knowledge imparted. It takes a mind like yours to disseminate and relay what we can impart, without blocking or dissecting the connection of source energy.

We welcome open channels to relay our discourses, so humans everywhere can connect and absorb our relays. At this time the heart chakra or energy centre is pulsating vigorously and many human souls are responding to the universal love vibrations, as sent from the Angelic Realms, to awaken the sleepers and re-ignite enquiry within others, who have fallen into despair and despondency. Our work purpose is to enlighten the earth world to their spiritual brethren, who come to greet them at this time of closeness and unity.

The armies of celestial force are converging in great numbers under the leadership of some of the greatest Cosmic Lords. Such power and brilliance is awesome in delivery and humans should know that these legions are sent with God's blessing, to bring the starlight into earth world affairs. No longer are human beings left to fend for themselves, they are being helped and cajoled, to step into the light vibrations at every opportunity, so the great transformation of the Earth world can proceed to its flowering.

Trumpets are sounded, flutes are played and bells are rung out to herald in this mighty energy power, which has the effect of purging all within its path. Welcome the legions of light and absorb as much light as you can into your being. Every light particle absorbed can help in strengthening and perfecting your light form structure, so you too, can join the legions in their procession to the Sun Star apex. The life energy is most strong and vigorous, and can be used to bring healing if directed with love and compassion. Light power needs to be attached to compassionate actions, to be truly affective and robust. Employ the legions of light in your earthly endeavours, and see the positive outcomes generated. You can employ and harness this power to use for good purposes, and bring benefits to all those you know. In your teaching and classes you can use intent to attach this light power to you, so your awareness can reach the legions of light. They will respond and progress your learning and understanding of God's kingdom and realms. My direction is to impart to you the usefulness of your connection, and to ask for your co-operation to become a spokes-person for the legions of light. We know you already are a channel for other light-workers and we want you to participate in the present activity to bring new minds into their flowering mode. The more you can teach about Angels and the use of lighter energies, the more you can show and relay the influences more easily, so many more humans can understand and attract to their own recognition, the nearness of personal Angelic friends.

Each human soul has a Guardian Angel or Guide, so it should not be an unknown concept or thought that a spirit entity walks with you, to accompany you on your earthly journey. Many humans on earth are Earth Angels themselves, but work in different circumstances to those in the Angelic kingdoms. If an avenue opens for them, where they can use their services in helpful ways, then Earth Angels will use the presented opportunity wisely, to further assist the light emitions of truth.

Truth about creation and existence.
Truth and knowledge of Cosmic Beings.
Truth of life existing in different realms.

I bring a lighted torch to increase the light around you, so communication is made easy. I thank you for this relay between us, to establish friendship and reveal to you that it is your light-being Alana, who has helped enabled my contact. God Bless you and keep you safe – our connection is established and our notes encoded…………… Haniel.

What do we know about Haniel?

Archangel Haniel whose name means 'Glory to God' is an Angel from the order of principalities. This is the third group in the hierarchy of Angels, and the role of the principalities is to be caretakers over all parts of the Earth. These Angels are empowered with the great strength of God, so they can have a direct impact on human affairs. They are empowered to move hearts and minds within all nations, to bring about change, for the betterment of the earth world. Haniel is depicted as a woman of great beauty and furthers friendships and pleasure. She can help you give 'Glory to God' by living at your highest potential. She is able to turn barrenness into fruitfulness, and can change moods from sadness to happiness and can help polish your skills and talents to master-ship levels, to fulfil true passions into divine magic. Haniel specialises in assisting the legions of light, so the Ascension of All Souls is forwardly progressed.

An Angel of Consequence

Chapter 21

HANIEL
Speaks again

We surround you with love and lighted presence as my fellow angelic workers are anxious to include your students in the golden hue of divine vibrations presently sent to you and your group, who are raising their awareness to higher realms. We are excited when including new members to our fraternity who show interest in all things Angelic. New students to the lighted realms of Angelic presence are eager to learn more, and become acquainted with their own Guardian Angel, who looks after them and their affairs. When all eyes turn upwards to spirit, we bask in the glow of admiration, which is received from earth dimensions, as this makes our work with the newly initiated, so much easier and greatly rewarding.

In times past many Angels have provided services to humanity and have made direct contact, with their presence known to gifted individuals, when the astral and etheric vibrations were in accord for such events. The laws of life have not altered, it is just the circumstances of the prevailing NOW times, which present a more advantageous time for close contact, and we always take advantage of positive changes where our work and influence is concerned. We hope we may add to your circle light by way of bringing our presences into your group setting. In doing so, many will feel the effects of the lighter vibrations and wonder at such enlightenment, for within the Angelic light there is always healing, and no human is without need for some help or uplift, in their own personal life circumstances.

We aim to assist and bring benefits to your group, as we are aiming to become inspirers to those who would be our willing channels. There is a need for many channels to operate for God's words and speeches. It is not enough to bring messages from loved ones, however rewarding and beneficial it may be, for also there is the need of God who wishes his children of earth to know him and his love. It is his love which has sustained life on your planet, but this has often been misunderstood by the very ones who should know the truth of eternal existence and creation. When the common man and woman takes naturally the understanding of the existence of Angels in a real and tangible way, rather than relegating this knowledge to mystical insights by the few, then can humanity rise in statue to the realms of their light-being consciousness, and become living proof that spirit resides in physical form and is exemplified in mankind.

Present humans are at last realising that they are more than just the physical kernel of their material form. Through your emotions and desire nature, your electro - magnetic field of vibrations, which is known to as your aura, scintillates most vibrantly, and acts as a filter for all outside emanations, from levels existing in time and space. From finer vibrations you receive influences and knowledge, but you as an individual and collectively as a race, do not have a uniform receptive mechanism, so it has been left to the few, to interpret as best they can, the relays from higher realms. Your history and your good books held by many nations, reveals the presence of Angels, for it is we as a race of beings that have been able to circumnavigate the restrictions of material existence, by operating on the streams of love and light. It is a paradox that humanity retains great measures of love within their beings, and it is to this love that we connect. There is no doubt that the general level of awareness within humans is being raised to new heights, so that more and more are awakening to divine revelations, originally seeded within their psyche.

It is this aspect, that with the right and necessary key-note of the present age, hearts and minds are opening and releasing all within. This great happening is the beginning of individual ascension and occurs when you recognise that the material life is only a part of your understanding, as you have perceived and sensed that there is more to know, and the pull of your spirit has brought you to the point where you presently are, in interest and realisation. You may have sensed things, and seen things, that were outside your understanding, but now you have found others who understand and can explain how phenomenon occurs. It is all because of increasing awareness which allows you to see and hear and know the reality of unseen life.

The pull of the spirit to know, is also the same pull that takes you through life, inquiring about eternal life and posing questions about the hereafter. Do not be afraid, for your spirit can never die and as one door opens and closes, so does one dimension follow on from another. The earth life is a great learning media for many truths are contained in earth living, if you have enhanced perception, and are able to make sense of the lessons before you. In to-days world many students gravitate to the mystical arts, as they are attracted to all things different and unexplained. It is the pull of spiritual influences that mark a route for the individual, which will show as landmarks, and are the keys to spiritual understanding and the higher revelations of God's kingdom.

All souls are heralded into the light, the moment they open their minds to the great revelation of all – that the God of your creation is the hereafter, the essence of all things, and it is his Angelic personal who are his servants in all aspects of creation, and it is our purpose to help and assist those who may need a helping hand to bring divine illumination to their souls. This provides buoyancy to that soul which enables spirits to travel into dimensional life. This ability of movement is directed by consciousness and does not only apply to those who are physical dead.

Indeed, in the present time of NOW, many humans are travelling during sleep and dreamtime, to view and experience for themselves, the dimensional realms, and this provides a humanitarian understanding for earth dwellers, for as you sow, so shall you reap. Universal Law in action is for everyone and is a perfect means to bring balance and harmony on every level of being. Know as we draw close to you, we offer friendship and ask for co-operation for our worlds to be more closely aligned. Then new friends can be made and loving vibrations expanded, so all may benefit from additional light and goodness, which may then be spread widely upon your earthly kingdom.

Until later my friend ……………….. Adieu

New Horizons

Chapter 22

Spiritual Gatherings

The powers assemble to wish you well upon your journey to an elite gathering of souls. Besides meeting up with many friends, you will enjoy the presence of high officials from the spiritual realms, who have come to lift the vibrations to a new and clearer level, where many advance minds and souls may connect into the starry realms where Angels dwell.

Yes it is I Haniel, who come again to connect with your thoughts, and be the spokesperson for a group here in the spiritual realms, who wish to work with you. We are also working with the higher officials, who will be governing the assembled group's activities during this time of closeness, for this is an opportunity not to be missed, as it is but a yearly joining. The officials of spiritual beings are the guardians of Earth's atmosphere and are the ones who stand steadfast in channelling energy to your planet, and who have continued to outpour the divine essence of God's will and purpose. Each and every soul who assembles to your gathering is able to carry the light and healing, direct from the source of divine intelligence. We are spirits empowered to further God's divine essence and we are preparing to empower many from your group to do the same in a more direct fashion, which will enable the healing light to be more powerful when administered to those upon earth, who are in acute need from suffering pains and physical discomforts.

The same administrations will also relieve mind-pain and bring greater harmony to personal thoughts, as the eyes of the soul will be encouraged to look upward, when the pull of the spirit increases substantially. We ask for your co-operation in this work which is of an essential nature, for we must step up the applications of the higher vibrations, to bring the effects to be more clearly visible.

From our place in spirit we can direct powerful energies, but the effects are governed by the receptivity of the targeted person or place. As many humans generally have raised their vibrations of awareness, this had enabled our ministrations to reach greater areas of world populations. With greater co-operation and involvement from earth inhabitants, who become Earth Angels by the carrying of healing light, we can do even more, to bring about the planets ascension into the lighted realms. With willing helpers we can direct our lighted healing to where the person of earth directs their intent, to help and assist their fellow man and women.

We attached our light and power to the psyche of individuals who are honest and reliable channels. These are also sensitive to the higher vibrations to allow us, to flow the power through the channel of their being and thereby reach the one who is most needy. We ask all of you who may not consider yourselves as healers, to attune to our vibrations and allow yourselves to be influenced. This way you will heal others without knowing it, as you will respond to circumstances as they arise, and reach out to the one who has come to you for help. The moment you put your hand upon another, the healing energy flows. Even being within the auric energy field allows the healing power to creep in, so know that when you consciously are used as a healer, by using hands to relay healing power, you are channelling our directed lighted energy, which has first entered you, via your heart centre and then is relayed through each hand.

It is you who become a transmitter through your own being, and serve the Great source of all, by attuning to the highest of highest levels. This gives a pure and direct channel for your directness of intent, and gives a greater sureness to your ministrations that will indeed be affective.

I leave you now in the glow of my words and directions for I know you will transmit this relay to all your friends at the family gathering. May the love and light of pure joy be part of each day of your living, so you can reach your high level of attainment in all that you do and say. Being a servant in the greatest movement there is, will bring you to the glory of existence, and the realisation of what exactly love is.

………………………….Haniel

Joining Hands in Co-operation

Gathering

We assemble at your hotel to see what arrangements your tutors have made. We are in contact with the Guides who are monitoring the events of your week and giving instructions to your tutors as to what is best for you and your needs. The energies themselves are beneficial to you and the healing taking place at this time is of a high order. So many vestals can pour healing light to the needy with some requiring just a little adjustment to their flow mechanism, in order to activate the healing directly and bring about substantial benefits, from elevating many hurts and problems. The classes of your course are designed to fine tune where needed, those aspects of your being that will serve you well. Each one has been directed to the class which will be most beneficial for them, even if they do at first think, they may not have made the right choice.

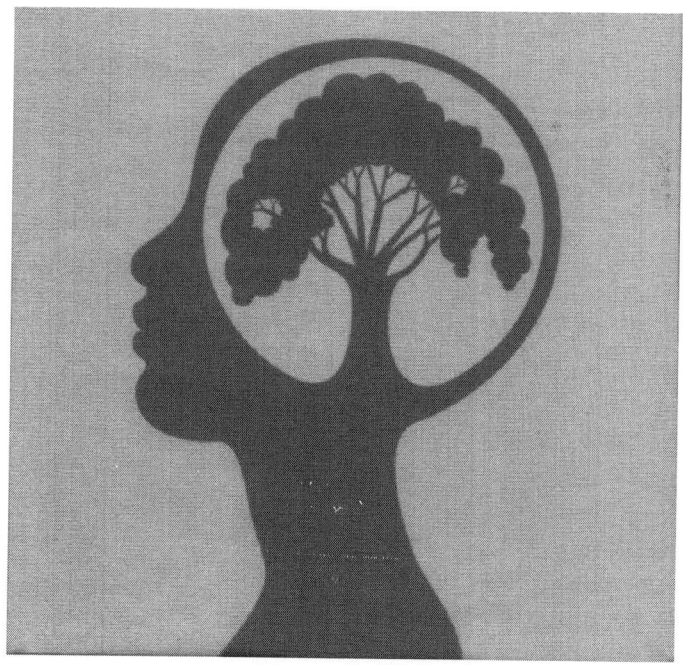

Chapter 23

Jeremiah – Old Prophet

I come to communicate that the old signs of religion are being replaced by new signs derived from old and ancient symbols used by the etheric and nature species. The crucifixion is being consumed by fire, because it symbolises a focus no longer relevant, as death and dying are obsolete, for signs of life and renewal are now more appropriate, and it is these images which require adoption of use, so as to bring the vibrations of life power more fully into individual forms. The symbol of the Sun is old and seeded by Ra the Sun God in Ancient Egypt and in Southern American civilisations. The Rainbow Arc is another symbol, being used to show the natural life of nature and creation, which brings renewal and hopefulness in colour to make a bright and colourful world. The old sign and symbol of the Tree is once again brought forward with a new concept added.

The tree roots represent humanity striving to reach the pinnacle at the group apex, which is representative of the base chakra's denseness and contained in an arrow shape, pointing downwards in the earth and this also forms the base of a crystal wand. As souls ascend through the trunk which houses the energy centres or coloured levels of ascension, they take the energy, to the tree crown which is another arrow-shape pointing upwards Once the crown centre is reached the branches spread out as a web, being the universal matrix, and it can be seen at the end of each tree branch and twig, a fruitful manifested pearl of wisdom.

These represent the culmination of wisdom which is symbolised as petals or pearls and drop from the wisdom tree onto the fertile ground of earth. This energy fall enters the dense material environment of earth-soil, to be absorbed by the many lines and tentacles of human chains, which make up the root structure of the tree of life. Wisdom energy is absorbed by the human roots and drawn up through the trunk, as the human souls rise in ascendancy and merge into the celestial universe.

This action completes the circular mechanisms of regeneration, eternal renewal and life in abundance. The pearls of precipitation contain the silver and golden hues of colour, that enrich the soil of earth to promote the nurturing of life and its living media of the tree organism. The more the silver and golden hues are absorbed into the living tree structure, the greater the colouring of the tree, which at present is changing its note of call, into golden hues of resonation.

It is the age of golden times and living that are bringing in greater enlightenment to humanity, and this will herald a peace that will spread globally. Countries and Nations will trade in friendships and prosper in wholeness and this will become a reality. The spiritual aspect of life will become important for all peoples, as values shift and old cultures contribute their ethnic highlights, thereby dispelling negative beliefs as they are improved by more acceptable and recent ideologies. Freedom and self realisation will predominate, and where possible, the life circumstances will open for the flowering and unfoldment of individuals everywhere.

The veil between worlds will be truly torn asunder and co-operative living of dimensional life will ensue. Glory and goodness will be the keynote of the age, to be heralded in as more pearls drop from the branches of the life tree and are absorbed by the souls of ascending humanity. The tears of Allah are indeed fertile waters for growth, as are the raindrops from heaven.

The Age of Aquarius is represented by the water carrier and it is the symbolic lady as the feminine aspect, who caries the pitcher of water wisdom into the Now and Coming Time. Water is an element of healing and when water flows vigorously the flow washes away debris that is no longer needed or wanted. Stones and rocks are shined anew to reveal hidden depths of colour and pattern. Know that through the coming age the outer shell of human form will be water washed clean so pristine colours, hues and shines can manifest their glory. Know also that many aspects of nature will also be refurbished after a thorough clean and shine, through water power and the earth world will glow again in glorious splendour.

The Mystic Tree of Life

The symbol of the Tree of Life has existed for eons and adopted by the Buddhist organisation as a peaceful image upon which to contemplate. With additional qualities bestowed upon this natural symbol, its power is enhanced and humanity uplifted to higher levels of awareness. The capabilities of human kind are endless and that also includes the higher evolved animal consciousness, as it can be seen that the animals of higher order are also responding to the lighter vibrations. Animals too are evolving their own mind sensitivity and that is why many humans empathise with all sorts of animals as they become more aware of the communicative capabilities between species.

The Communicative Process

Chapter 24

Nazarene

I come to you with great love as I know you have been aware of me and my influence. I use you as my spokesperson as I mentor a number of your group, who have expressed the fact of being aware of my presence in their mind linkage and auric emanations. I confirm that my presence is not always sought by everyone, but sufficient of my devotees exist in your group, to evoke my personal presence.

My light shines for all, but those who acknowledge me are able to perceive my vibrations and follow the lighted energy to where healing and enlightenment are sourced. I come with my mother who you know as Mother Mary, for she also presents herself to you and your colleagues. She advances angelic healing and assists in personal healing concerning family individual relationships. My presence this time is to oversee the channels of trance, as it is necessary to perfect the lighted mesh of communication, so that those who can connect into the web of light, do so knowing that their connection is sound and robust.

My light shines brightly on all who show interest to me and my cause of fellowship amongst all peoples. My spiritual brother Buddha opens his avenues also, to accommodate the flowering buds of humanity, who cannot accept my light because of indoctrinations from zealous preachers, who have misconstrued my message to earth, and have prejudiced those very ones who need me most. You know that I am part of your White Brotherhood of Ascended Masters, and the aim of that fraternity is to positively influence humanity to follow the spiritual pathways.

As many of the Ascended Masters are representative of differing ideologies, they influence those who would think differently to main stream understanding and accommodate all who would aspire to lighted realms, but cannot understand the interpretations of scriptures given by earth men. In spirit we all come together in one group and pool our light, for together we cast our light and that of the Christ Light. My influence can be felt more greatly when a few earth disciples assemble in common thought and aim. Many who are undecided, and sit on the fence, may say they do not know me, but they are the ones who have at some time in their life, cried out to spirit for me and my father to provide help and assistance. We have responded, for we help all humans, who are in need and do not differentiate between belief systems, as all are children of God and all avenues lead to my father, and there are many paths that lead the way to him.

By recognising the Great Creative power and the existence of the Great Mystery or Celestial Seas, you acknowledge the Godhead and reality of prime source energy. Within all creation there are entities of energetic form, which govern sectors and sections of God's kingdom. Many humans upon earth are experiencing an expansion of their energetic form and can now perceive the great beings who reside within the Cosmic Spheres. It is these Great Beings of light who are the builders of form and Guardians of existence, and as the human race ascends to the lighted realms, more and more will see the Angels of Light and their ministering hosts.

We who are part of the White Brotherhood draw close to earth living, for we act as the forward team of helpers to the Ascension process, affecting individuals and the planet. Because this is a cosmic affair on many levels, the happenings upon earth are important, and necessary understanding is needed, so all aspects of ascending entities and the Ascension itself, is seen and understood by everyone.

The human race, are the blessed children of God who were given a paradise environment to be their homeland. The experience of seediness and evolution of forms, through the cyclic nature of earth has both aided and hindered the Earth's history. At one time we did not think the human race would survive, but many here in spirit assured us that humanity were able to absorb the light and many spirit personalities have re-incarnated to assist the human race, to raise its vibrations, so it could ascend at the time of the changing era. While my light is acceptable to many, and I offer a pathway of progress to all who follow my light, there are other avenues that offer the same service so everyone is accommodated.

Do not think that anyone is left out. What your faith-men tell you is not true – all humans are loved equally, saints and sinners alike, there are no preferences – only universal laws which apply equally to all. If you are righteous, helpful and give service to others, you are living a good life of productive service. You know the differences between negative and positive vibrations, moral rights and wrongs, and know also that light defuses darkness and turns negativity into inert substances which are non-harmful.

Follow lighted ways, and follow my way if you are able and feel comfortable to do so. Rewards are unimaginable and love abundant. I lead many souls to the higher pastures in God's Kingdom and invite all who hear my words to join me and be my servants on earth. You too can shine the light of spirit, to lead the uninitiated to home pastures. From there, we in spirit will take them further, so you know you can be assured, that more souls are saved and taken into the God's house and home.

May God's blessings be with you always

The
Nazarene

A Shinning World

Chapter 25

Guides and Contacts

I was meditating to bring the white light of spirit into my heart energy centre, when I perceived a crystal within the heart cave shinning brightly. This act brought communications:-

Old Prophet - JERAMIAH

I come on the crystal energy line of your connection to communicate this night. You have been aware of me as you described me earlier, when immersed in the process of my connecting stream. The crystal heart intensifies the power and increases the effectiveness of light to hail your call. There are high frequencies within your group and this can be used for astral travelling, or as a general energy torch within your locality. The expansiveness of your thought processes takes you into the universal realms of the Great Cosmos, and out to the edges of time where time ceases to be.

The great cosmic beings of light energy are holding the resources of dynamic power in check, to allow the debris of non-compatible substances to disintegrate and dissipate. Without fuel to feed such substances, the dying embers of the last period are but of short duration, and soon will be no more. Fresh material will take their place to flood the cosmos with new energy and light, so renewal and reclamation is achieved. Alpha and Omega will again hold hands and unite in union, being the pair of galactic heroes of your cosmic space. Together they renew their vows and promise to keep faith with their children and homeland. The celestial sun shines brightly on this pair as they honour their heritage once again, and direct their vibrations to planet earth.

A Buddhist singing bowl sends vibrations to the heart of celestial space and calls forth the Angelic Host to attend this gathering. Glory on high, Glory, Glory sing the Angels as the high octane power is sent up from earth dimensions. It is a clarion call from Earth to the high officials in spirit to remind them that some humans are able to connect to cosmic sources, and act as Earth Angels, to call the Legions of Light to assemble in gatherings of equal measure. We come to answer your call.

Captain Gillion

My name is Gillion – Captain Gillion of the space ship Santa Maria. We give female names to our ships because a female has nurturing skills and looks after the children. Our space ship is home and security for those who live within and need nurturing in care and safety. We are propelled by plasma and can seem to materialise and de-materialise by earth eyes. My mission is to co-ordinate the armada of spaceships arriving in your quadrant during 2012 from the Pleiades constellation. We are humanoid like yourselves but differ, being on average seven to eight feet tall with larger eyes and elongated heads.

We have been evolved for much longer than humanity and are workers for the Cosmic Christ who directs us to the Planet Earth for the Ascension process. We come to witness the transformation of energies and help in the process, by forming an arc of ships around your planet. Our energy is lighter than earth energy but you can see our ships as energy forms, like a cigar shape or elongated bubble. Evolved humans can see us subjectively and may be objectively, but to see us visibly with your own eyes, we would have to lower our energy ratio to become more compatible to the surrounding vibrational rate. Our minds can reach your receptive human minds, as many are newly open and receptive to our transmissions. We are NOT ANGELS but living entities from another star system that your astronomers can recognise and mark.

We have consistently spent our time with great effort for humanities benefit, as we are custodians of advance learning for many in our universe. We know of the Christ Light as it is this energy that has played its part in our own evolution and anyone connected to this power, knows it is most beautiful and fulfilling of powers, as it is connected to divine source and the great creative power through love. Our space personnel assemble to perform a service to humanity and come physically close, so our energy can be much stronger. We will have greater control on how we work when directed by the Great Earth Angel who is a cosmic force and manages the power of harmonies around Earth's atmosphere.

Amongst our personnel we have individual members who are expert sound and thought transmitters. These experts work through the earth vortexes on your planet and connect to shamanic or hermetic leaders, who understand the earth and cosmic connections. Many of these earth beings have lived in solitude like hermits, just guarding these vortex channels, which are classified as special areas or scared land sites. Know that through reaching living earthmen throughout the globe, any special instructions and knowledge will reach each nation via the ethnic communities that provide prophecies and portents.

You are not alone in your hour of flowering, as many from universal sectors are focused upon your planet and the life ascension in becoming. Your planetary flowering produces a perfume most stupendous and it is this energy release that those who surround your globe are waiting for. It is a most beautiful blessing of receipt given for services rendered, as the perfume is of a glorious hue that has special properties for galactic servers. It sets up a new resonance of call from your planet to attract the high council of intelligence. This council is the galactic and cosmic think tank and are the overlords of existence. They have the power to bestow the sacredness upon a planet, and bring the core vibrations into the central control of the cosmic source.

Formations

Marie

Dearest beloved, we surround you today to bring you upliftment and healing as your services to us are rewarded by our service to you. We are aligning your energy more harmoniously so you will notice the aches and pains are absent, and the twitching of limbs are silent. We will take you deeper in the altered state so you can experience the nearness of divine energies and the joy of love that is present when connecting with the Angelic Host. The Angels are in abundance here this week of your gathering and are being recognised by many individuals within your group. This is the confirmation that we are present and assurance to all, that we have the group energy controlled, so the many activities of linking to spirit forces can proceed without disturbance. We aim to smooth the waves of connections, so everyone has an enjoyable and memorable time. Our love is ever present and so is healing that you all can freely download into your body-forms.

Alana

I am Alana come to talk again. I see the excitement of your activities and the great light sent skywards to us in the spirit realms. It is good to be able to laugh at yourselves, as spirit is always greatly pleased when mirth and laughter are generated as this lifts vibrations to goodly levels. It is like adding octane content to original fuel, to make it of an extra or superior fuel and you have certainly generated plenty of superb power, which we can use for your finale presentation, when four trance mediums perform together in unison. Our side is excited at the prospects and I am viewing the preparations taking place from spirit side. You are indeed fortunate to have such a dedicated leader, who is highly regarded by the spirit workers who are attached to her energies and light. She is a jewel amongst you and you have done well by attending each year, the sessions she has arranged for the family gathering.

Amongst the attendees are those that you can administer to and we arrange such opportunities and conversations to benefit all involved. Your work is noticed by many who record your progress, so carry on as you are doing and enjoy the rest of your stay. This is your reward for all the work you do that goes unnoticed and unrecognised.

Grey Cloud

I am Grey Cloud, who you are not familiar with, but I have attended your family seminars before, and you have at one time become aware of my energy, although you were not consciously able to recognise that energy as me. Now you are more enlightened, you can understand that my presence is more acceptable and you can now channel my thoughts sent your way.

At this time my people, the star people assemble in abundance as your group light draws our race to you, by the many connections the energies make between the different worlds. We come to greet you and make ourselves known, because we are able to use the collective energies for our personal and group use. I am here beside you, as you are unusually calm and tranquil, and this affords some introspection. You are entering a new phase of learning which you will find interesting, for you have been using techniques and channel automatically without fully and consciously understanding how these lines of communications come about.

This information will be useful to you for teaching purposes and in an ever scientific environment, there are new initiates who will understand their own ability more fully, if they are given insight on how the mechanism for attainment operates. My job is to instruct you on power and energetic manipulations, as it is something that many of my people understand well, for we grew into this understanding as part of our original culture.

In today's world only old cultures and religious practise continue to teach energy formations and its applications. Many eastern Indian Yogi's retain the advance knowledge, but have yet to apply this knowledge on a grand practical basis. We use sound and resonance to generate energy forms, that can be used productively, and we will show you the patterns that are produced by such means. It is the prelude to star formations that geometrical patterns prevail, and this process is replicated in other applications of energy uses.

And you will develop the awareness to see actually the fine processes that go into such phenomenon. Rarely do living humans understand the intricacies of behind the scenes workings, to bring about co-ordinated, extended and affective physical phenomena. Anything such as speaking, gyrating, singing and dancing are physical phenomenon's and the standard of such manifestations will be governed by the amount of energy available to produce the level of quality exhibited, together with the willingness and receptivity of the incarnate soul, to lend itself for such work.

**A Human placed within
a Merkaba Star.**

Communion

Chapter 26

Angel Star Healing

The star power holds the golden and white rays in harmonious balance so when healing is given using the six pointed star symbol, the energy flows in equal measure. The Angels come on the pink ray of universal love, to surround the patient and healer, as both are placed in a larger Merkaba Star structure, to allow the healing power to flow unimpeded. The Ascended Masters and Angels look on, and are represented by the presences of power beings, of Melchizedek and Kwan Yin, often seen as Jesus and Mary energies.

The white light flows from the crown to the base centre with the pink energy flowing to the heart. Together these vibrations produce the pearl pink ray of loving healing, pervading the whole body structure. As the healing energises the hands by implanting the star energy upon the palm, the healing force directs the auxiliary power to connect upon the head, shoulders and solar plexus. By placing hands upon the shoulders, this allows the white light to flow down the spine, which opens the lower chakras. This allows the pink ray into the heart and out into the auric field. The glands of the human body are balanced by this healing and the throat, heart and solar plexus energy centres, are fortified for spiritual work. The Solar Plexus is the central point where the earth energies meet, and those lower points of healing are used for grounding and earth balancing to the human structure, so that the knees and feet when energised will support in robustness, the frame of the human being, to become a sentential of light upon Mother Gaia.

This healing is not only for the physical ailments, but opens the gates within the human framework, to flow the light of spirit to all levels of human life and living. The lower framework of bodyform needs to be strong and solidly strengthened, to keep the upper trunk in a good working format, as this area houses the transmitter and receiver sites. The lower centres provide the physical fuel needed to operate the higher portals to spirit, which in turn open, to allow greater light and healing to enter into the human body. The more the human vessel is opened, the greater is the capacity, to receive and transmit all that is necessary, to keep the physical bodyform robust and working correctly to enable the spiritual centres to function at their best.

It will be found that when working with Angel Healing, the intensity of healing increases, and the effects of the healing will prove to be of a greater intensity, being of a higher and finer power, and as a result, emotional and physical reactions may strongly manifest. Deep emotional release is a symptom of Angel Healing which provides cleaning and clearing of deep seated problems and blockages, to free the flow of energy systems within the human bodyform.

Even with humans who show no external problems, the chi energy system may be sluggish or blocked, and by releasing hidden debris, migraines, headaches, tiredness, and mental slowness will disappear, to be replaced by a more clear and energetic formula. Brightness and sparkle ensues, with clarity of mind becoming a symptom of positive healing from receiving such treatments of Angelic intervention. You may ask 'Why is Angel Healing any different from other healing?'

It uses the same energy of lighted colours, but with Angel Healing the vibrations surge from lighted personnel, who are known as notes of starlight. They have unique properties of special fineness, as they come on a flow directly from source. That is why they are finer and more potent.

Beforehand, these energies were used sparingly and selectively, as these powerful surges could cause unknown upsets. At the time of NOW, it is the Angels and Ascended Masters who are drawing closer to humanity, and as a result can influence best via the healing processes and treatments. The clearing process enables the channels of reception to open, and many who are called to be mediums of communication, are serviced anew and made ready for greater clarity of working.

The more light and love that can be spread around the earth world, the more it enables others to open and become God Receptors. When hearts, minds and bodies are made whole, the understanding of God's Kingdom will become second nature to everyone, and by connecting to divine sources as individuals, you will know that all are as one connected to the divine, and personnel conflicts become a thing long forgotten.

Everyone loves Angels, there is nothing you cannot like about Angels unless you are afraid of light, so the more light that can be spread to those in darkened circumstances, the greater the lighted fields become, to welcome the Angelic host into the Earth Kingdom, so all areas can be flooded with healing, love and light.

Melchizadek, Kwan Yin
together with the Angelic Host.

White   -   Angel Gabriel
Gold   -   Angel Uriel
Pink   -   Angel Chamuel

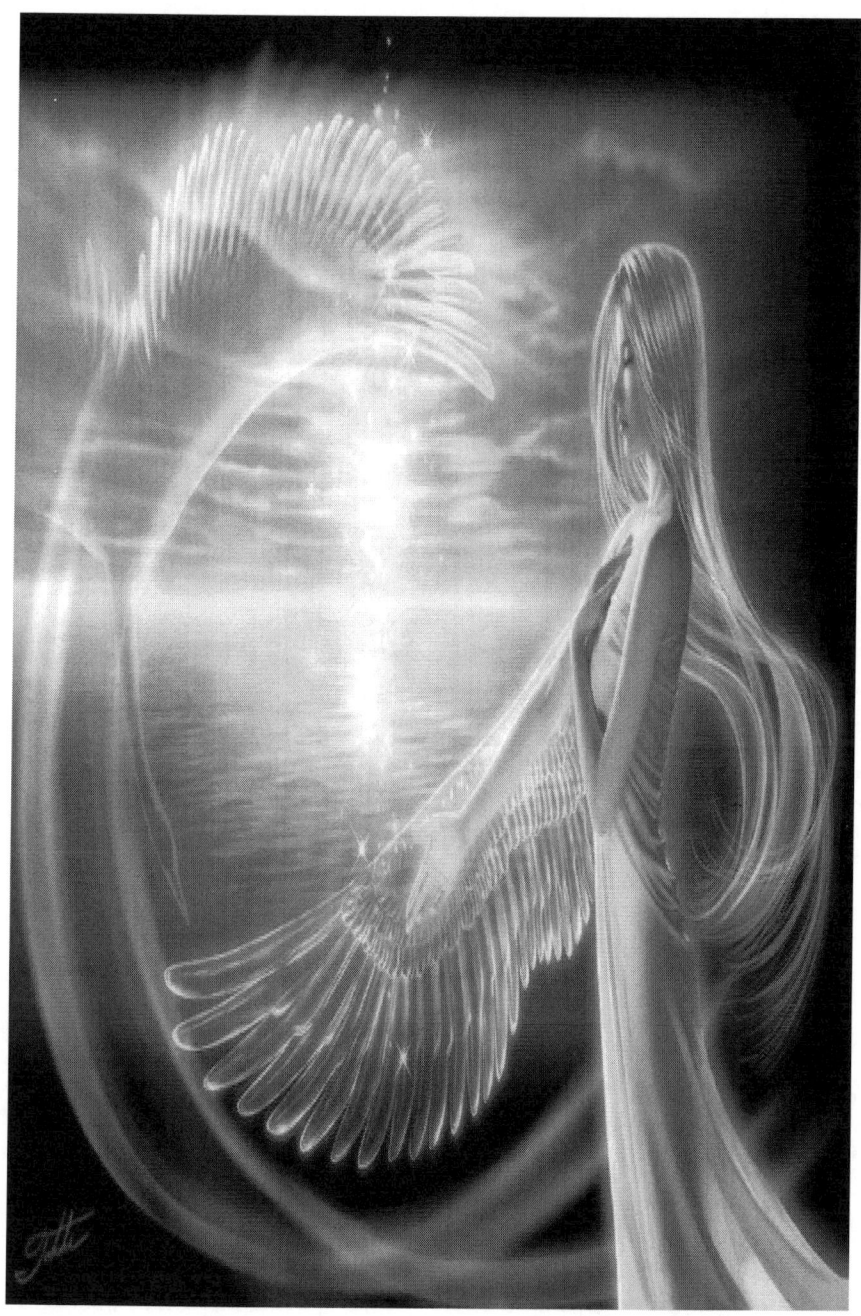

Chapter 27

A New Dawn

A new dawn may start with the rising sun, as it ascends upon the arc of vision, whether in the north or south hemispheres of the earth globe. The best view is seen when in the open countryside, as the landscape is laid out in its natural formation and the effects of the rising sunlight upon the land, can manifest in some unusually light reflections, as the darkness is chased away from the sleeping terrain. The sunlight wakens an otherwise sleepy land into a new days activity, and brings warmth and clarity of vision to the working environment, wherever that may be, upon the lighted part of the globe.

Each day evokes a new dawn upon the land and signifies the light time of activity, as from the time of darkness when at night the land and much upon it slumbers, so that it may restore the energy reservoirs within the physical structures, ready for the next dawning day. And so the cycle of daily renewal continues in a rhythmic manner, as part of the workings of the earth's life and the earth creatures living environment. The Human Being is the king of beings upon the surface of earth's landscape, and has established a living life to dominate most of all other earth's life forms, as the human had risen in intellect and knowledge, and the race has circumnavigated the globe, so very little is unknown and untouched by human hands. It seems that the human species had saturated its world and is now facing a dilemma regarding its next step of evolvement. Many humans have recognised that there is more to life than the physical existence, and it is to the spiritual life they are now turning.

Anyone who begins to question life at its fundamental level is a person who has turned a corner in their mental evolvement, and has started to question their own held beliefs and ideology. A New Dawn has arrived for a new approach, a fresh approach, a different approach. A New Dawn offers new opportunities that may have far reaching effects, for the pathway of life opens broadly and seems to be without boundaries to impede or suppress. All options are open for experimentation, so ways may be found to forward the human race in a direction not thought of before, and often it is the simplest and most logical of progression steps to take, which will lead to a new dawn of knowledge and enlightenment. The human race has achieved is zenith and has begun its homeward journey. Now humans can see the interrelatedness of all things both seen and unseen, for the viewpoint is such, that it affords a backward glance at the avenue trod in achievement, where the energy formats are shown and displayed. By re-examining past achievements the motives and the motivations can be examined also.

It is a great learning tool this re-examining, because many lessons can be learnt from past undertakings, as seen in a new light. By being more enlightened today, you can see the mistakes of yesteryear and know why they are mistakes in today's understanding. It is like having wisdom in hindsight. An action taken at one time would not necessarily be the same action you would take again, if the same set of circumstances arose. You have achieved a maturity of wisdom now, so you know things today, that you did not know some time ago. Life is a great teacher and many humans learn from their life experiences, but some never do, for they seem unable to grasp that their life is anything else but a continual rounds of selfish pursuits. When all humans are stopped in their tracts, and asked to consider what they are doing and for what reasons, then many would be surprised at the answers or non-answers given. The New Dawn of consciousness arriving for each human being is the realisation of the self, as a cosmic being.

A spirit and soul that is everlasting, housed in a temporary material body made from earth material, in which the spirit and soul may reside, while it experiences the living life upon earth, and all the lessons offered to it, by the earth life and environment. When an individual realises that it can start again from the next new physical dawn, then the living life takes on a new meaning and a new purpose. Changes are taken with renewed vigour, knowing that the focus of the living life has changed, to one of brotherhood, friendship, loving services to others, caring and sharing with others, who are wiling to reciprocate to you. Being charitable to encourage more to find the light of new living, so all humans may benefit from peaceful ways and learn how to accommodate the differences in people, as you accommodate the differences in other things, seen as varieties of species whether Animal, Vegetable or Mineral.

Varieties and differences are all around the living life. Look at the flowers and vegetation with its variegated forms. Look at the animals as seen in the many varieties within the same species and different species. The world is made of colour and so everything in it will be colourful, as it is an expression of the life giving rays of colour, brought to the earth world for its building of forms and cyclic workings of nature. Know that a New Dawn in human life signifies a major turning of the race's focus. More and more people are becoming lightworkers and are gravitating together in forceful groups. These are the future leaders of society which can be found in all countries and all nations. Light is spreading at a fast rate, and each country is becoming affected, for the common man is questioning the present governing regimes, and standing up for their human rights. The common people want to decide their own futures and are voicing their cry. Fighting for recognition consumes the interest and sets the focused sights upon an achievable goal. Use the New Dawn to change the present into a better future, so all future Dawns may radiate greater light upon this world for generations to come.

A New Dawn

Chapter 28

Britannia's Influence

The eyes of the earth world are watching the heavens, as the New Dawn of your current historical period opens in fullness to the divine energies of the cosmos. The hierarchy are preparing for the grand opening ceremony, as you upon the earth world prepare for your Olympic Games to begin in mid-summer. It is not coincidence that the major countries of your world are sending representatives to attend a civil gathering, which is the largest and most prestigious of all events, as it carries worldwide acclaim and recognition.

It is a fact that people of every nationality will assemble at the solar plexus centre of your world, and this event should not be overlooked as the force of power from the uniting of peoples will be a significant springboard, for the spiritual hierarchy of beings to make the brotherhood of souls more prominent than ever before. Your City of London is old with wisdom and carries with it a solid structure of open heartedness. From this centre, justice carries the equalising scales, as Britannia holds her shield and sword to show her strength and valour in equalising harmony. Dignity is served by the upright backbone of a female who carries justice and honour upon her shoulders. Beside her stands a lion who is a protector, a sun-soul who guards and glories in the female strength, which is tempered by compassion and understanding.

Britannia rules in more subtle ways, as she has gathered many cultures to her bosom, by giving sanctuary to many who flee persecution. The ruling governments have failed to see the strength in Britannia and have sidelined her to the history books and memorabilia, but do not make the mistake of dismissing her altogether, for she has powers hidden within her spirit and soul, that may surprise everyone. Britannia is simmering for the time she will rise again to prominence and centre stage, for she may be battle weary and a little tarnished, but she has learned from experience that diplomacy takes you far. The lady is not for turning, for always Britannia is facing westwards, ready to fight her way through to reach the pelicans of peace. The sea is her friend for often the sea has been her moat and saviour from unwanted advances. She pauses and asks her people from within her shores to look at her covering and soul.

There is no need to biker from personality differences over spaces of living, for the land is for all to enjoy. Those who have the ability and energy can climb the hills and mountains, stroll over dales and lowlands, swim or paddle in lakes and rivers and dry off in scented meadowlands. The beauty of Britannia is breathtaking, especially in springtime and early summer. The temperate climate of your island can be changeable, but what a delight there is, with so much variety to clothe yourself in a kaleidoscope of garments, to mirror your surroundings. Such is the scope open to many human beings, who have the perception to see beyond the obvious, and delve into a more meaningful relationship within the natural world of your habitation.

With the influx of nations at the time of your Olympics, more colourful personalities will invade the islands of Britain. The air will tingle with delight and the airways will be thick with commentaries. All eyes will be focused upon the few, who are the chosen ones from each nation, ready to excel and do their best within their chosen field of sport. Some will win, some will loose, but the taking part in such an extravaganza will surely stay in the memories of many for years to come.

Look at the faces of the young and see how they envy the more able. They will be inspired and try to shine their light upon the masses, but may choose different ways to do so. Such are the opportunities open to every soul who aims to further the living life and grow in maturity and knowledge, to enhance their own potential through soul growth. There is no need to look for adversity in order to learn by sorrow and misfortune. Look to the positive ways that everyone can grow by working for their brothers and sisters, whatever colour, race or gender. Learning from each other is a good way to advance personal understanding of co-operation and harmonious relationships.

Make friends, not adversaries. You will need many friends to help you, when the hour of advancement arrives. You will ask for testimonials, you will ask for recommendations, you will ask for support and find out who are your true friends and associates. True friends are not jealous of each other, for they recognise the abilities and talents of each other, and are prepared to acknowledge the attainments gained by perseverance and diligence. Friend's glory in the differences of each other, for everyone is unique and have their own pathway to follow.

Being envious of another only stifles your own progress for you fail to see where you could shine and miss the opportunity that awaits you, because you are absorbed in another person's life and consequently overlooking your own. There are times when you should look to your personal self and be 'selfish' for the right reasons. This applies to individuals as well as countries for each must retain its individuality and uniqueness. Such is the colourfulness of the human being when the soul light shines and begins to attract to it, those other beings which scintillate in harmonious accord. The lightworkers everywhere are drawing together and beginning to filtrate into the battlements of governing and civil managements. Britannia is supporting the greenness of all disciplines, so her colour remains unchanged, and her power and energy can once again rise to heights long forgotten.

So to the supporters of colourful interchanges, look and listen in the coming time, for many will experience an expansion of their present understanding and knowledge. They will take on the newness of the present age that brings a fresh approach of co-operation between peoples, the colourful people who make up your world. Make your land the best and beautiful to become the bright star it is, so Britannia's light may act as the lighthouse to steer others true.

Welcoming Newness

Chapter 29

Healers of All Souls

Ten of us were asked to sit in a circle and attune to the healing power. We held hands and asked for the healing energy to be passed via the healers to the recipients in order to circulate the energy around our circle in a rainbow of colour. Rainbow colours had been seen earlier and described as coloured fountains, so we knew these energies were around us. The energy could be felt by tingling in the hands, as vibrations of healing energy pulsated through each and everyone present.

I became aware of a clocked gentleman. He showed himself with his hood covering his head, but with plenty of room at the sides, so his face could be clearly seen. He had mid-brown hair slightly wavy with a clear skin and beautiful blue eyes, which radiated out with concern and compassion. I knew he was sending healing to us, as the glow around him became radiant with intensity, as I could feel his energy being sent to our group. He reminded me of pictures of the Nazarene and I felt the tingling response shiver down my spine as this thought occurred. Great Healing power emanated from his being and I was overwhelmed by his love. Another healing lord presented himself who was adorned in a full length robe with a waistband. This person reminded me of a Cosmic Lord. He or she had a golden headband with fair straight hair cropped short at collar length. A Golden disc shape was upon the headdress which gave the impression of a glowing aura, which in fact was demonstrated to me as a reflective shield to aid the direction and force of healing rays.

This was Haniel who I have seen before. Haniel is female so it could be that the healing energy requires both the male and female energies, to bring balance and wholeness. This was confirmed by the colours of green for wholeness being present and the introduction of yellow for greater vitality and vigour. Haniel is an angel from the principality realm who acts as a caretaker over earth nations. Principality Angels are empowered with the great strength of God to have a direct impact on human affairs. They are able to move the hearts and minds of nations, to bring change and betterment upon our earth world.

When I next looked, I saw a cloak around Haniel with a pointed hood. This changed into a Golden Eagle which soared up high as if to overshadow the group. I took this as a symbol of power of the Great Spirit connecting to the divine. This connection enabled the realisation that we can live in the realm of spirit, at the same time as remaining balanced and grounded, within the realm of earth.

The Eagle feathers are considered to be great healing tools for they have been tried and tested over many time periods. They have been used by native shamanic peoples, to cleanse auras in aiding healing balance and wholeness. The Eagle reminds us all, to gather courage and soar upwards to overcome the mundane levels of life, and so refine the personality aspects by reviewing ourselves beyond what is already known.

By attacking personal fears, our souls can fly with the Eagle in the airways of the Great Spirit. The Golden Eagle brings great enlightenment and illumination to everyone who walks in the shadow lands. A freedom spirit can appreciate beauty, as it can love the shadows as well as the light, as it sees beauty in both, and when the Eagle flies even higher, we can know and experience, the joy of our hearts desires.

The picture of the Nazarene in his cloak reappeared. As the healing group closed the meeting by sending healing thoughts to those written down in the healing book, then Jesus opened his cloak and encompassed us all within his auric being. A warmth and peace enveloped us all, and for a few moments no-one spoke. This afternoons healing gathering had been a special experience that many had recognised as profound and unique. Most of us registered this power is some way, and some of our healers recalled seeing light and rainbow colours, which were very evident throughout this afternoons healing gathering. Our closing prayer offered thanks to spirit and the healing guides for what was in fact a most precious gift of insight.

The affect of this afternoons experience remained with me for hours afterwards and later that evening I was able to keep calm, cool and collected when giving a clairvoyant message to a gentleman who had been greatly affected by the sudden death of his friend. This tragic experience had in fact awakened his enquiry into spiritual matters, and that was how he had turned up at a demonstration of clairvoyance, where his grandmother had informed him that she knew how he had recently been feeling. She was helping him further his new found interest. The loosing of a close friend had shaken this gentleman and knocked the stuffing out of his being. As a consequence he was re-examining his own life and values. His grandmother was able to tell him how his recent feelings were expanding his new awareness, so that in the future his life could take on a new direction for himself and his family. Patience was required, but the knowledge was given to this man, that the changes he sought would come to pass, when he had acquired the confidence to put his new thoughts and ideas into action, from gaining the knowledge he was presently absorbing.

God works in mysterious ways,
His wonders to Behold.

Golden Healing Energy

Chapter 30

Healing Specialists.

The healers in the spirit realms are many and varied, and of particular interest are the equivalents to the paramedics, who are first on the scene to any accident or unexpected event, when an injury or sudden death occurs. There are teams of healers who specialise in sudden death events, which can occur at any time and appear to be unexpected to most incarnates, who are relatives or friends of the departing individual. Many spirit teams work in troubled areas of Earth, where conflict reigns and violence and accidents are rife. Other spirit teams work in more civilised and developed countries where domestic and natural deaths occur from everyday events, illnesses and unexpected happenings, which may seem unexplained, but occur because the karma of that individual has decreed its physical ending.

Healing teams are like scavengers who pick up souls from sudden death regardless of cause. They are able to view the life remit of an individual, so it is known to them, that the call from the spirit of an individual soul, is ready to leave sometime soon. The teams lay in wait, so they can be ready to pick-up a soul, the moment earthly circumstances align for spirit delivery. This way the earthly person is whisked away from material life in a flash, without pain or suffering,, as one moment they are here on earth, and in the next moment they are in the spirit realms. It is this suddenness of change, which often leaves remaining earthly folk in emotional difficulties, as the impact of the sudden death happening is abrupt and final, with no warning or forewarning. Adjustments are required to accommodate the absence of the physical nearness of a loved one.

Time serves to lessen the pain of parting, as the realisation comes of the continual existence of life after physical death. For those who hold the burdens of grieving long after the normal time of adjustment, there are the places of earthly healing centres who offer healing for body, mind and soul. At these centres, many are cured of things which trouble them, as the mind and body adjusts to the healing soul, who is suffering from past effects logged within. Many ailments are cured by spiritual healing because they are linked to deep seated traumas, many of which are unidentified, because they go back beyond the present life to past existences. Not everyone understands or wants to be regressed to find out hidden problems, which they may or may not have already identified. Many humans take the view that it is best to leave well alone those things not fully understood, because they are afraid they may unearth something unpleasant. This is a naïve approach, as all things unknown are at first viewed with suspicion, and it is only when pioneers have braved the avenues of newness, that others will follow knowing the way is now safe, or can be tackled in an understandable method or manner.

The Healing Angels have their allotted tasks and undertake a monumental workload. The Guardian Angel of each individual is the closest spirit entity to a living human and when there is interaction with the healing Guides and Angels, it is the Guardian Angel who initiates the contact, and allows the nearness to benefit the circumstances and conditions prevailing. Sometimes when specific healing is needed, the human is guided to a healing centre by some unknown force or influence, which is usually the Guardian Angels influence operating through the higher mind of that human. The human thinks it is their own idea, but rarely bothers to check, as life circumstances have a way of overtaking present thoughts, with new feelings becoming all consuming, as the healing power works its magic and wonder. There are healing Lords and Angels at every healing centre and many are now arriving from cosmic sources to aid the earth population in the refining of physical bodies, to coincide with the Ascension process which is current and on-going.

As new energies are lighter and more refined, so it is that the healing processes are refining the cellular human structures to become receptive to current cosmic forces. This will allow more healing to flow through the earth healers, as they align as receptors to the Angelic Realms, and become the facilitators of lighter healing energy. More humans will encounter the second sight and rainbows will appear more frequent to be seen externally and internally. Colours will appear brighter in nature, and more and more humans will come to appreciate flowers and grown vegetation.

Sparkle and glow will become more frequently used words of descriptions, as the flow of light within metals and earth manifestations becomes brighter and more vibrant. Love will vibrate as notes of radiance, and it will become a measurable power source. Love is the greatest power on earth, and so it is in heaven, as it is the cohesive force between the manifested and un-manifested. God made the human being in shape and form, but man did not emerge as a living entity until God gave man his breath. The breath of life is the greatest gift that God bestows to a new born child, and when it is time to return to spirit, the breath of life is returned to God. When a human soul returns to God, he gives man life in his house and home. His Angels administer his kingdom in all dimensions, so do not be surprised when you see an Angel, for one is never far away.

All Angels can bring healing but some are more specialised than others, as they have elected to undertake specific work which in human life is replicated in the many avenues of service. That is why if anyone asks how best to serve God, then it is to serve fellow humankind in what ever manner is appropriate. Helping and assisting are ways of service that can make a difference to someone else's life. In doing so, you act as an Earth Angel, as service is God's way of giving and spreading love.

Embracing the Light

Chapter 31

The Creative Force

The creative force within nature comes from the source of universal power, which brings the energy of the cosmos to the planets and stars within the material universe. As well as the essential ingredients of divine power required by those who inhabit the unseen realms, the Great Cosmic Beings and Angels of which only little is known, are the facilitators of such cosmic ingredients. What is known is that these beings of lighted presence are the very intelligences that impinge on the earth world, to bring to us who are mankind, the wisdom of the ages, and to our earth planet, the renewed energies of celestial alignment.

Often a lighted entity has to clothe itself in a familiar garb to become recognised and accepted by a certain human. This certainly is the case when a non-human guide or mentor is influencing a human mind, and will take on a human frame and personality for identifiable purposes. It is known that human minds are narrow in their acceptability and find it difficult to think outside certain ranges of propagated thought patterns. It takes a brave human to publically acknowledge something unconventional or taboo. Individual thought is given credence and is often encouraged, but not always readily accepted by those whose minds and understandings are not so open or wide. There are many present organisations made up of people who have cleaved to an ideal, which over time has become outdated or non applicable because of changed circumstances.

Any view put forward which challenges the prevailing format of acceptance, is seen as hostile and threatening. This gives rise to rejection and rebuff from those who feel uneasy, because they do not want to face the truth of change, as it makes them feel uncomfortable and unsafe, as there are no reference points. A universal truth is set for all to adhere to, regardless of locality and the greatest truth present, is that of continual change or movement. It could not be otherwise, for if there was no change, life would not evolve and continuance and progression of life would atrophy, and loose its life force of animation.

The divine power from source which many call God is the true essence of being. In manifestation or existing within the invisible worlds, this divine power is present and acts to bring life and movement into and out of forms and structures. Those forms that become materially manifested, are those forms clothed in the densest of matter, so that the light of spirit essence can only be seen by the clairvoyant eye, and not by the physical eye of the material being.

The inner clairvoyant eye can see the energy surrounding a manifested form, and can view the flows of vibration or resonation which make themselves visible within the clairvoyant faculty. Thus it can be seen ahead of manifested time, that certain occurrences are forthcoming. To a normal human without understanding, such knowledge may seem magical and mysterious, but to a metaphysical student, it would seem quite natural and normal. Thus we have science to thank for delving into areas of boundary knowledge and expertise. The shamans of old, the old crones and wise men and women detailed in earth history books, all told of the wonders of magic and mystery knowledge appertaining to nature and natural events, whereby foreknowledge was known. Predictions regularly came true or facts were given before they were understood and accepted by actual proven material fact.

The mysteries of creativity are many and varied, and it is to the unseen helpers of the earth world, that gratitude should be given for the many services provided to Mother Earth, and to those creatures residing upon her surface. Little does the human race know that they have been assisted in their evolution, by the myriads of elemental creatures, whose stories have been told many times, as captured tales for children and contained in fable storybooks.

The great cosmic beings are those who have been engaged with fundamental creation of the planets and star systems. They are mathematicians, engineers and cosmetologists extraordinaire. They are supported by the best and brightest of Angelic Helpers who are universal craftsmen, and like an artist, have creative skills and talents all their own, which adds to the colourful and extraordinary variety of what amounts to manifested life. The answers to creation are contained in a plant which begins its life as a seed within the ground. It has planted itself within the dark earth which when watered and warmed, begins a process of germination, whereby a seed sprouts and a plant begins to grow. It can do this, as the seed contains an element of divine light or energy, which provides the mechanism by which it recognises germinating conditions, so when the ingredients are all present, the seed will begin its growth.

The seed will follow its blueprint, which is contained within its original code of origin that denotes its form and particular variety. This is what distinguishes an oak tree from a willow or a frog from a human being. Eggs or seeds are present in vegetable and animal life forms, and it is by these methods that newness and creativity come into being. Eggs and seeds may need fertilising and by this act many permutations of species can evolve, and become beautiful adornments upon the earth planet. Original seeds are stamped with a blueprint, which will replicate each time renewal is activated. Such is the process of continuance of life of the material and physical form.

Where fertilisation occurs, the combination of blueprints follows progressive evolution, so a form may become adorned with varying colour combinations to add multiple variations to a species. The spiritual essence of an entity can never die because it is reabsorbed into the etheric body often referred to as the soul. The etheric body resides in its own right and provides the energy framework of an individual. This structure interpenetrates a physical form but remains intact when that form is eventually vacated. The mind is not physical and remains as consciousness residing in the soul being of a human, who has been released from their physical bodyform. Hence the etheric body form becomes the non-physical body once the physical frame has died, but the mind retains the personality or greater aspects of its developed mind, for the consciousness is ever expanding and seeking new experiences. The awareness of consciousness is retained, for when spirit life registers, a review of the physical life takes place of the earthly existence recently lived. The self becomes its own judge and jury because it is its own regulator.

God has given the human soul, the ability for self progression towards perfection of beauty, goodness and truth. The internal regulator of the spirit is the human soul's consciousness, which distinguishes the good, the not so good, and the unwanted aspects presently under review. The spirit life will afford further refinement of the soul's makeup or the soul consciousness may take the decision to re-incarnate into another physical life. It may transpire that the physical arena will provide greater opportunities for the soul's advancement at the rate that soul decrees it will undertake. The pull or force of the spirit and soul to reach its Nirvana is different for each one, so it is up to each individual to determine which life it prefers to exist in, according to its soul-life journey and the coverage and extent to which soul-travel and progress has already taken place. Thus the personal remit of every human spirit and soul is to decide for itself, the progressive rate of its own journey progression, and which world will best suit its purpose, as it makes the trek towards the fulfilment of personal soul life goals.

Chapter 32

Meditation and Prayer

As children you may have been taught how to pray, and the archetypical figure of a child such as Christopher Wren in his night shirt, kneeling by his bed praying, is a picture encased in many minds. It is when young that you may have been taught to pray, for your parents, brothers and sisters, and to bless your house or home. By praying in this way a child sends thoughts of protection to his or her home and its occupants, to protect and preserve in safety, all that's held dear. When growing, the child is somehow taught to pray for others, but not necessarily for itself as to pray for oneself is deemed selfish by mentors.

However when a little older the young persons desires or wants, stretch to going to a particular college or university, and their thoughts go out to attract this desire of want in great intensity. Often the prime objective is never achieved and the second best choice comes to fruition instead, which turns out to be the fulfilment of ones needs and not ones wants. This proves that unseen powers have been listening in, and have manipulated events to provide fulfilment in ways not envisaged, but in ways of natural occurrences, designated for the best fit. This is often the first stage of recognition, of the Laws of Attraction, for as one thinks, so it becomes.

As an adult the many ways of prayer and meditation may be studied, and it can be found that the meditative process has healing and beneficial properties, resulting in the relaxation of the physical body and the calming of the mind.

Those who study Yoga or Buddhist ways may appreciate the power of the breath and the control of breathing practices, to further the meditative and contemplative process. Certainly many can claim that by meditative practice the inner place of quiet can be reached, where the inner voice of ones own spirit can be heard. It is from this place of inner sanctuary, that many beneficial aspects to the self and spirit realms can be accessed. For those who have need of removing blockages within the psyche or unconsciousness, which are the causes of adverse fears, phobias or physical bad habits, they will find the altered state achieved, by going within the self. This can access the real causes lodged in the past realms of life hidden long ago, and forgotten within the cellular memory of a person. It may be in the present past life or beyond in past lives, but the point of causal input, will be accessible through the mindset, by those knowledgeable as facilitators to unblock the lighted lines from personality to soul.

It is through the meditative process that the place of sanctuary or stillness can be reached. From this place other doors can open to other dimensions, and students may find themselves exploring various avenues to see where they may lead. By understanding the energy makeup of the physical body, and its portholes of input and exit for the travelling consciousness, a student may try out the various modes of meditation. First the relaxing of body and mind enables the freeing of the self from everyday cares and troubles.

There are many programmed discs and tapes for relaxation. These take the student to places they can relate to, which calms and relaxes both the physical and mental vehicles. The next stage is guided meditations which are not meditations in the true sense, but exercises in altered states of awareness. These guided journeys are destined to foster greater awareness and enhanced clairvoyance, clairaudience and clairsentience.

The student who is studying self-development of the enhanced senses, can operate in conscious mode more effectively, when dealing with communicative aspects between the unseen and seen worlds. The real journeying into unseen worlds and contact with spirit sources, comes from astral travel or out of the body experiences, where the consciousness via the meditative process, is able to leave the physical body and travel to other realities. This can be achieved by exiting via the Crown Chakra (Top of the Head Centre) or Alter Major Centre at the (Back of the Lower Head where it joins the neck). Yogis use this exercise as second nature, for they have been trained in these exercises since young, and for them it is completely a normal process and proven manner of connection. It is through such contact with spirit sources that wisdom is transmitted, via experiences or by dialogue, or inspired thoughts for record.

There are many humans who receive inspirational wisdom though the altered state of deep concentration, providing a light trance gained from practiced meditations. The levels of altered states can be accessed more easily and directly when experiencing meditative techniques which have been studied and employed. By using the mindset in a controlled and positive manner, the thoughts used in prayer become incantations, to fuel the manner in which energy is relayed and used. The understanding of universal laws, brings into play the cause and effect of actions, so as you formulate thoughts into a prayer or incantation, the emotional thrust gives strength and purpose to the vocalised missive. Like attracts like, and energy follows thought. This is a truism. The meditative state brings quite and peace to troubled minds and bodies, and allows healing to mend affective parts and restore the energy balances into harmonised wholeness. So if you want to access wisdom yourself, you must follow the meditative processes to find your own personal connection to spirit sources. Soon you will find directives received that are full of knowledge and wisdom. You will know the truth of your source from the calibre of information you receive.

Never doubt that you are unworthy, for the God of your creation chooses every channel willing to become an advocate for his work, regardless of whom or what they are in personality. The criteria for choosing spiritual workers, is the willingness to serve the light and the love of the great source of life itself. In serving this way you become a light-worker and facilitator. You work with the lighted brotherhood, whose aim is to serve humanity and guide the race to its potential apex, so Earth and Heaven may join as one. By learning to pray and meditate in a positive and meaningful manner, you open yourself to receive all you could possibly want to know and more. You will find yourself travelling to places you never dreamed of, viewing scenes you never envisaged and meeting people of spirit, who are more alive than you ever thought possible.

Your understanding will widen exponentially and never again will you judge a person upon sight, for you will know that all is not as it seems. There are vast areas of untapped knowledge to be explored and you will not be satisfied until you have attempted some measured revelation. Positive thoughts will form your day into one of construction, so your waking moments will be focused upon the meanings of existence and life in all its forms. You will welcome the chance to converse with masters who are able to provide information to answer your many questions. You may even volunteer to become a member of a task force, if you are a person who wants to be a part of your physical life changes.

What starts out as thoughts, becomes a plan. Plans become blueprints and blueprints become prototypes. Etheric structures which are the blueprints can become concretized and be brought into physicality when many thoughts, prayers, incantations and aspirations are packaged into powerful energy pockets.

This forms part of the creative formation which humanity has yet to fully grasp, for your environment is made from your collective and individual thoughts, so it up to you as individuals and as a race to fashion your surroundings in all its aspects, to become as you would wish it to be.

Be wise and teach your children to pray and meditate in a correct and positive manner, so many more facilitators and lightworkers may join in God's Army of servers. This will bring your planet and its peoples into the greater light of heavenly being and improve conditions of life and living most beneficially. Many more people will become co-operative and realise that they cannot operate without one another. No man is an island so the saying goes, and indeed no man is. Each human is a part of a greater whole and interrelates with all that is around it. This connection may be to other peoples, animals and aspects of nature being birds, trees, flowers, hills and mountains.

A man who is connected to his garden or to natural places in general, is a fortunate man who understands the earth energies, and the elemental vibrations that are so uplifting in their cyclic nature. These natural manifestations of life bring much colour and fragrance to the surrounding atmosphere, and to those human beings, who are the gardeners or tend such places, bear witness to the beauty and peace that these places can bring.

At times when magical atmospheres can take hold to energise the moment, is when the subjective senses open to absorb and respond to such stimuli. Then the connections to sublime sources of spiritual excellence is experienced and felt, in such a manner to be indisputably the product of God's presence in form.

Projecting Thoughts
to the Physical World

Chapter 33

The Spiritual Surgeon

A friend had reserved a ticket for me to witness a spiritual surgeon give a demonstration. I arrived in good time for the 7.30pm start. The man Mike explained he had been impressed by spirit thirty years ago and had been directed for spiritual development by being introduced to certain people who had in turn directed him to others who could further his understanding and personal development. Early on he had been asked to be the channel through which a healing guide could work and provide healing services, as he had been told many would come seeking help and healing. After explaining the evening's format and the procedure to be followed, Mike allowed himself to be entranced by his healing guide Peter, who then took over for the next two hours of healing practice.

It was explained by Peter the healing guide that he worked without having to wear spectacles, whereas his host Mike could not operate without them. This was confirmed by Mikes partner who was present and organising this event. Peter worked with spirit doctors, surgeons, nurses, healers, energy technicians and lightworkers totalling fourteen in number at each session of spiritual healing. The first patient who was treated was experiencing back pain after having a back operation. Peter the spirit surgeon invited two observers to attend of which I was one. We were asked to place a hand on the woman's spine and I could feel an intense warmth envelope the area. While I could not see anything with my physical objective eye, I did perceive with my inner subjective eye.

I was able to see and know that unseen hands were operating on the mid-spinal discs and clearing away adhesions from the spine itself. This was confirmed by Peter as well as attention being given to freeing the nerves away from the spinal area as the adhesions were dealt with. After treatment the lady reported that the pain previously going down her legs was eliminated as her discomfort had disappeared. She seemed a bit dazed in her surprise which was unusual for her, as she was the church president and usually vocally active.

A man patient also had spinal problems and was suffering with uncontrollable spasms occurring because of misalignments of commands sent out from his brain. Peter explained this and that was why he started with healing the head, so as to correct the signals directed to the body parts. Healing was administered to the spine with the assistance of the hands of two more observers. I picked up clairvoyantly that he was being fitted with a spinal sleeve that wrapped around the spine to help straighten it. Later, Peter the spirit surgeon stated that the molecular structure of the spine was being altered to become malleable, so it could be strengthened and that an etheric rod was inserted to straighten the spine and once straightened, the molecular structure was adjusted back to solid, with the rod removed and thereby a straitened normal posture resulted.

When the patient lay straight upon the healing bed, Peter laid his hands upon the emotional centre and explained he was checking the progress of his work through this centre, as it contained and revealed the emotional reactions of the body. This man needed further treatment, so he asked him to sit down for a little while so spirit could continue working upon him, and asked him to be prepared to have another session a bit later on where final adjustments could be made. While this man was waiting to be recalled, I was asked to take my turn as a patient. I was suffering from lower back pain linked to my hips which manifested as a continual dull pain.

I knew I had been overdoing physical lifting recently, due to the circumstances of earlier weeks, where I had also been under intense emotional stress following my father's recent sudden death. One healer had her hands on my head while Peter the spirit surgeon linked with the observers hands upon my hips and then subsequently moved to the centre where he asked one of the observers what they could feel. 'It's like a bolt joining the back and front' the lady said. 'Yes' said Peter, the spirit medics are working on the base of the spine. Then he placed his hands on my pelvic hipbone. I could feel a line of warm energy flowing between my hips and back in a figure of eight. I could feel movements of energy all around my pelvic area. By the time they had finished I had forgotten the pain as it had disappeared. I was still a bit stiff and tender in my movements, but the continual discomfort was gone. I was impressed and thankful, and most grateful believe me.

Being doubtful as humans are, I waited all of the next day to see if my discomfort would return. I can thankfully say it has not. My hips are free from the continual pain I had been experiencing and my back and pelvic area feels free from stiffness. When I think of the six months I had been attending a chiropractor to adjust my spinal misalignments, it just makes me so thankful that spirit can effect such healings in such a wonderful unassuming manner. In a matter of fifteen minutes spirit treatment has made greater inroads into rectifying my personal health problems, than six months of previous therapy involving physical realignment treatment.

After my healing session, there was a man patient who was having trouble with his eyes. He was suffering from blocked tear-ducts as he had dry eyes and couldn't cry. He also complained of blurred and fussy vision at times. When he was receiving healing, more than one spectator was aware of a brilliant white light being directed to him and many vocalized what they could see or were aware of. The spirit surgeon Peter told us, he was clearing the tear ducts and proceeded to give healing upon the solar plexus which is the emotional centre.

He joked that now the man would cry buckets when anyone upset him or he became overemotional, so he should not complain when this occurred. Normal service had been resumed he told his patient, and the man smiled gratefully as he thanked him for his administrations.

That evening was full of enlightenment and many who were not normally clairvoyant knew or saw physically, the actions and effects of those in spirit, who had assembled as the healing team to carryout the spiritual operations and healing required. As I was a beneficial recipient, I can only recommend the actions of Mike Smith the medium through which his spirit healing surgeon Peter operates………www.spiritsenergy.org.uk

Clear Seeing

Chapter 34

Many Feathers

My power has been great for I have many sons and daughters to show for the loving of my years in and out of physical existence. I have taught many in addition to my nearest kin, for I share my knowledge with those who will listen and are prepared to receive. My greatest love is for my Lord Creator, who has rewarded me by giving such bounty to my life remit, to show me and others that working in service to God's wishes and commands, is pleasurable and bountiful in all its aspects.

Embracing lighted thoughts, word and deeds increases light emitions, and the inner light within all beings can only shine more from such expanded efforts. Never is energy purposely depleted if service is given in Gods name, as automatic replenishment of the love energy is activated, with bonuses aplenty. The secret of success is to flow your will, with the Great Lord, who in love will take you to places where your best interests are served. There maybe no rhyme or reason to events that you can see, for you are not party to prime causes; only to the effects are what you can see, as they register upon you and you react in consequence. You could say, you are tested by the great powers, but those tests are always positively induced, to gain the best efforts and highest values from your personal capabilities.

It is because God loves you and seeks to see you progress to your greatest potential, that challenges are set before you. It is up to you to make decisions to rise to the challenges of life, if you so choose to do so. To confront challenges head on, can provide the quickest route to achievements of enlightenment.

You are not obliged in any way to take up the challenges you encounter, if you feel unworthy or unable at this time to expend the necessary focus or energy required for such endeavours. Someday however, you will decide to tackle many aspects of life, that you are required to overcome, and choosing the time and place is one of choices put before you. Putting off today what is presented to you, will only delay matters, which of course is your choice also. God gives us the necessary challenges when we are ready to deal with them, as a way of passing to the next stage of development, in understanding and soul growth.

This is how I was given many feathers, to denote the many deeds carried out and my achievements within my earthly lifetime. I was raised to embrace life in all its aspects, and I found that loving was most pleasurable and enlightening, as it opened many hearts to me, even those of my enemies. I could look into the hearts of others and see their fears, for they lacked the greater understanding that comes with knowing you are connected to the life source, and your life is as eternal as the cyclic seasons in nature. By living life of fullness in the moment of now, you reach up to your highest ability and give of your best in every circumstance. This is the best you can do and achieve, and if you have carried out your duty and responsibilities in this manner, you carry no reproaches for any lack of worth.

You have achieved confidence because you have given your best, so any criticism from another, falls on deaf ears, as you know you could not have given more or done anything better than what you already have done. Be proud of your accomplishments and strive always to learn more, so in your personal growth your abilities are increased and a wider span of effects, can become manifest when you administer your gifts and talents, to benefit those within your life circle of friends, relatives and near ones. I offer my advice, so you too can gather many feathers from your living life activities. Life upon the earth is short, so make the best of your time to influence as many as you can..........spirit guide

Chapter 35

Newly Arrived

I have today visited a beach of pristine white sand with blue waters washing the particles so clean and bright, that it is hard to believe that such things exist. It is so tranquil here, just the sounds of the rushing water as it ebbs and flows in regularity. The sunlight shines endlessly here, just warm enough and bright enough to feel comfortable. I am wandering alone upon this beach immersed in my thoughts, as I remember my earthly life amongst you. It seems strange that I can now choose to be alone or with friends, just as the mood takes me, and all the while I feel safe and secure in the loving embrace of Gods love and beauty.

The God of the Heavens is a presence that fills every living thing, and brings to the mind and senses, a well-being which is difficult to describe. It's a bit like being in love and seeing everything around with new and bright eyes, for in a sense it is a new awakening, to behold such beauty and magnificence. I am walking leisurely to the glass temple upon the small cliff above this sandy bay. It sparkles from the sunlight bouncing off its reflective surface. This temple draws me, as I can hear faint music being played and this is inviting.

As I draw nearer I become aware of light-beings or angels walking through the entrance. I join them as they are assembling for a discourse by some high official. I don't know the person by name that comes to speak, but everyone is so amenable and helpful and without talking in loud voices, they initiate the process of directing me to a seat by mind blending, which translates as speaking to me directly by internal thoughts.

I see that there are many gathered here and amongst the Angels of light, are other human souls also gathered. I am aware of a companion who has now joined me, he is my Guardian Angel. He is nice and friendly and knows me so well. It's like having the best companion ever, for he can be a friend, confident and teacher, all at the same time. I think his name is Sabastipol, but I call him Sab as he is very accommodating to my needs. He makes me laugh with his playful nature, particularly at times when I may be thinking of serious things. It never ceases to amaze me, that I only have to think of him and he is present.

Sab shows me a game of compartments which somehow has bearing on how I think, as he is training me in ways to master the thought processes, which will enable me to travel and manoeuvre at will, like him. I have done quite well so far, and have visited lots of places. I have spent time with my dog that came here ahead of me, but I leave him with animal friends when I want to be by myself. The animal enclosures are wonderful to visit, and it is an exciting time, when human souls come to fetch their pets for pleasurable reunions.

There was one little girl who came to find her goldfish. Sure enough we found him in a large aquarium that housed a multitude of other fish and creatures. When Lizzy put her face up to one of the large aquariums, the little gold fish swum up to greet her, just as he had done when she was on earth. He gave her so much joy and entertainment that Lizzy never forgot him, so he came to thank her for making him individualised, and able to live in the spirit realms where human souls reside, and where he could live also and continue a happy existence. I have never seen a little girls face light up so brightly, as when Lizzy found her goldfish Sunny. It may seem strange to say, but they had a conversation, and then Sunny swum away to be with his fishy friends. Lizzy held my hand and I took her back to her mother, who was waiting patiently watching the joy emanate from both of us.

Now I walk back across the white sandy beach accompanied by my Guardian Angel. He follows a few paces behind me and answers my questions as my mind formulates them, in this walking meditation by the waters edge. I look out to sea across this moving ocean and feel the gently warm breeze upon my face. It is lovely and so comforting, that I look forward to my sleep. I will be taking some time out for personal growth and contemplation, as I need to reinforce my present experiences into mind awakenings and light configurations. This is part of the colour dream programme I am experiencing, which brings clarity and focus within this new world. It brings strength to the light body of my present being, which is clothed in the latest fashions of multi-coloured silk and velour. The fabrics and colours here are so much brighter - it's like being on holiday and taking vacations one after the other.

My love is given to all the family I have left behind. I will try to describe my experiences as best I can when the next open session allows. I know you are always ready for receptive duties but it is a case of aligning the energies when they best suit. All beings need activity and rest, so for now, that's the way it is for me, as it affords a regularity of events which is familiar, comfortable and makes me feel at ease. All is well here. I am at peace.

God Bless……………..B.

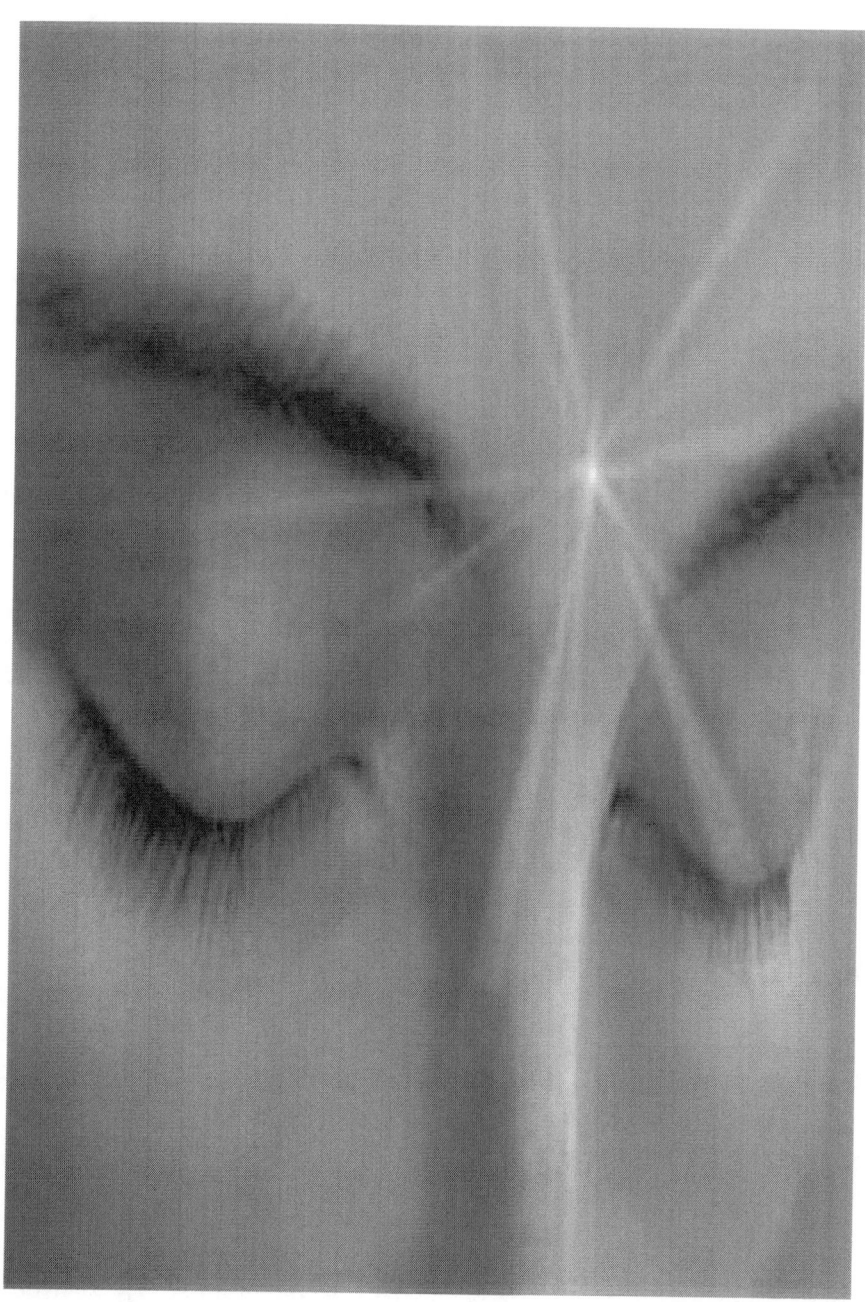

Chapter 36

The Awakened Mind.

The student of awareness may attend a development class for the purpose of becoming more aware of the spiritual realms and the knowledge of spirituality encompassing philosophy and truth. The student may have a particular goal in mind, perhaps of becoming a psychic or spiritual worker. It often comes as a new awakening when the avenue towards spiritual progression, brings milestones of perceptions, which enhance the widening of topics and subject matter under investigation. Since the object of a spiritual working clairvoyant and channel is to prove survival, then any proof of life existing within the unseen worlds, is a revelation to record and discuss. The sensual awareness of the physical mechanism each human holds is worked upon, to evolve a super sensitivity, which is both a blessing and a responsibility.

Many students first complain of a tight band around their head, like a bandana being tightened, which feels uncomfortable. This is quite normal as the pituitary gland within the head has begun to work more effectively, with the activation of the super-senses, and just as any body muscle is worked to a more effective level, it follows with feelings of aches and pains afterwards which express's the work carried out by under used sinews. The glands which receive new commands from the mental processes to work in specific ways, come to register within the physical body, and this is expressed as a symptom of a band of tenseness. This headache is often referred to as the psychic band, and is often registered by new students when they first take up meditative and psychic exercises, for the purpose of mind expansion.

Since mental exercise also involves chemical and energy changes, it stands to reason that the physical body will register different and new movements in some way, to make the consciousness aware of such changes. New students may also suffer from stress around the back of their heads and necks and along their shoulders before they become versed in meditative techniques and psychic exercises, which after a while become second nature to the progressing student, who learns quickly how to relax the body and still the mind. What students become aware of most notable is that the physical body is also an energy body, and therefore consideration is required to harmonise all the energy centres within the physical framework, in order to balance the earth and cosmic energies, which are used during the earth life experiences. Individuals may have to consciously adjust their mental energy alignment, according to their physical pursuits and mental thought actions, together with their emotional responses, which may be either positive or negative.

A practicing student with some understanding, can prepare themselves for coming events, when they know they may require added energy for a performance, or require protection if they anticipate contact with some adverse atmosphere or person wielding negative vibrations. Without this foreknowledge and preparation, the reaction to negative influences could be harsh indeed, and may have severe consequences resulting in physical ills and hurts. Life experiences should be dealt with in such a way, that unwanted influences are not stored or logged within emotional or mental vaults, but are released from the various energy layers. This preserves a neutral or positive energy being. If a human likens themselves to a light bulb, which emits energy and light of a certain frequency, then you would see the draining effect of the glow from that light bulb, if and when affected by energy sapping devices. A human body or Energy Being is similarly affected, so precautions are required to preserve the level of light vitality within, as it will affect the performance of that being, if energy levels are below par.

By being aware of the current needs of your energy body, you can prepare your energetic regime each day and for special occasions. This is particularly important for any practicing student, who demonstrates spirit contact through their mediumship ability, as such demonstrators are energy conscious, and can only work the communicative channels when energy levels are sufficiently charged for operative use. Many aspirants do not realise this fact, and wonder how information is forthcoming through the dimensional airwaves.

An awakened mind is one that knows the mechanics of energy manipulation and can use the available power of current vibrations positively and beneficially. The awakened mind also knows its limitations, so when communications are not as accurate or as powerful as desired, it is because the energy mix is not potent enough, and a greater bank of energy is needed for a greater and clearer transmission. An experience medium operative can connect to cosmic power, and use the higher vibrations in a direct manner, like plugging into an outside energy source. This reflects the advance nature of that individual and their spiritual progress, when understanding the part a facilitator plays in the practical performance of communicative activity between the spirit dimensions.

An awakened mind is an informed mind, so it can function at its best and most effective. Be sure to awaken your knowledge of energy uses when opening the communicative airways, so all those involved may exchange effective dialogue satisfactorily. There is great joy when communication between the worlds of life is made, and this invites other energetic beings to listen into the dialogue, so that enlightenment of communications between dimensions can be extended. Communications not only flow to human souls in the spirit realms, but to elemental beings in and near to the earth environment, who come to assist humanity in this time of ascending consciousness, so more knowledgeable mindsets can influence many unawakened minds, to open and see a whole new world. ....Sister Marie

Mind Expansion

Chapter 37

Forthcoming Changes

My beloved daughter, I surround you with love for your control and perseverance during this time of spiritual activity. You have reached and received healing during this time while living through a space of undemanding time, so your energies are balanced and revitalised. The atmosphere is charged with positive ions so you can tap into the energy vibrations anytime.

When rested, the mind clears and reception ensures. I come to talk to you about the new dawning of your coming Age. Many humans are opening their receptive centres and are beginning to grow their light within. The outward changes in life and society no longer bring worry or fear. Many humans are becoming optimistic as their outlook is changing and fear is replaced by more positive notions. Their view is a focus on the more simple and clear aspects of home and near relations and the family members of each group are forging closer ties, as they realise that together there is greater strength than operating alone.

More and more souls are seeking the meditative arts and all things mystic and psychic, so your developing groups are increasing. As more around you become awakened and the enquiring mind seeks solutions, you will find many students attracted to your circles of light. The elemental kingdom has begun its assault upon the dividing veil separating the seen and unseen worlds. As the Fairies, Gnomes, Elf's and Imps are clothing themselves in nature's adornments, to bring greater density to their forms, in line with the construction of the plants and trees they inhabit and tend.

The call of the vegetative kingdom is fierce as the blooms and harvest of nuts and fruit are abundantly spread as never before, and the contact with human beings becomes ever more frequent. At every aspect of expression, whether at sunset or sunrise, the human mindset is opening to the beauty and brilliance of nature's land. This is not something new, but the awareness and sensitivity is more acute, and it is a new awareness that is arriving, as the cosmic energy takes hold, to allow the human construction and constitution to flower in its own right. A human youngster goes through a rite of passage to adulthood, and so too, does the race as a whole, go through the portal to a greater awareness, to attain the clarity of life and being. It is like a New Dawn, as upon a new day everything is bright and clear, as optimism shines for what may come.

Hold hope and optimism in your hearts, as it is these attributes that open your receptivity. Everyone is feeling and sensing more than they have ever done before, and to some this new sensitivity is confusing and stressful. These are the people that require the healing vibrations to re-align their changing energy, to a more compatible mix commensurate to their changed surroundings. All areas upon your planet earth are changing vibrations, with some areas being re-aligned altogether, into a different land or sea mass. These changes are part of the cyclic changes that have occurred in the past, as the globe undergoes an axis shift. Your sun emits sun blasts that affect the galaxy in total.

Your scientists are knowledgeable enough to know which areas should be abandoned prior to seismic activity and climate changes, affecting the livelihoods of humans engaged in large scale agriculture. Areas are affected by climate changes as part of cyclic re-alignments and this is a pattern in the present time whose changes brings structural adjustments to existing areas, known for their long-term production and activity uses. The time for change is upon everyone, and will affect individuals and groups in different ways. Some will move physically, others will change outlooks, occupations and partners.

The way of living will change, as many will need care and consideration, by those who are more able, and by those who have the means to help. Many who feel isolated will be gathered into groups, for in the many, there is greater strength and resolve. The ordinary man and woman will speak out and want to be heard. When many feel the same, and decide to gather together, with their voices united, they will send out a call to be heard.

Co-operation is the key to advancement in most cases of endeavour. Loving your neighbour by serving where you can, brings a positive light into the many lives who participate in such ways. Happiness is assured if you work and play with love in your hearts, leaving harmful and fearful notions behind you. All things negative will lose power when your focus is turned to the lighter and brighter aspect of the living life.

The New Dawn will bring greater challenges in the short term, but the rewards will be significantly beneficial. Freedom has been fought for throughout existence and passing freedoms have resulted. Real freedom is the ability to do and go where your heart takes you if this does not harm any other or bring adverse circumstances to others. You cannot have real freedom if it is at the expense of another, for you are short changing yourself. Only by giving of yourself in unconditional love will you free your spirit and soul. Then you earthly experience can be undertaken without fear and hurt, as you will operate in your light vehicle, and your glow and shine will be seen by all who witness your being.

Love is the greatest power in heaven and on earth. Test its power for yourself. All who hold this love in abundance are immune to the petty hurts of everyday life. You are the stronger and more vibrant of being, as you wield the transforming power of lighted love in the service you have elected to give for your God creator, who has sent you to administer to those not so enlightened or evolved. Be compassionate, be understanding, be patient and be kind.

It is not easy to give service to others who do not respond with thanks but unconditional love is the way forward, for at some future time, everyone faces a time of need when services such as you can give, will be the very thing needed…..Nazarene

A Sunset

Chapter 38

Your Guardian Angel

At times of introspection we examine parts of ourselves which we rarely view. We are so busy living the daily earthly life that we do not give due attention to the part of us that dwells within. If we did, we may find a more meaningful expression to our lives, as the inner self points out the greater depth and expression to events and circumstances, which are presented to us for attention.

At a quite time of introspection, our Guardian Angel draws particularly close, for he or she surrounds us with a protective sheath to guard our emotional exposure, when we unearth something sensitive within our being. We may not realise it or even be aware of it, but we are examining parts of our soul quality, and as such this is a very delicate area which is highly sensitive, and when openly exposed in examination our vulnerability is acute. This is why our Guardian Angel draws near to protect us at these times, for as we delve within to a greater degree, we open out inner light to shine more brightly.

This greater shine is like a calling sign to those agencies in the unseen world that would use light power for collective purposes and assume that when such light is emitted, it is ready to join with the greater lights of illuminated presences to enable celestial movements, formations, regenerations and divine communications. You as one person are in the process of refining your being to become a better vessel for God's light. You are not ready yet to give of your lighted essence, for you need to refine and build your strength to become an active light-worker and healer.

When you have managed to attain a working state, and have harnessed the necessary knowledge and skills to manipulate your light being, then you can begin to send the healing light out for collection by higher sources to use collectively. In the meantime your Guardian Angel will act as your protector in all aspects of your physical, etheric and light bodies, and will personally assist in the transmission of light power when the time comes for you to consciously work in this manner of generating and sending light to the greater world. However wishful you may be to wanting to help others and to serve your great creator, it is necessary to grow in understanding first, and to know about the ways you can be of help and assistance. By understanding the mechanisms of light emissions, you will become a better transmitter of such powerful energies, and in doing so become more effective with your conscious thoughts and your connective healing ministry.

There is a difference between general light power and specific intended light power. General thoughts and prayers generate general light vibrations which gravitate to a pool or energy bank. This volume of latent power can be used by healing agents when and where the needs are great. Often when prayers are sent collectively by a group or groups this kind of healing power is generated for such uses. This can be important where a natural disaster has occurred and large amounts of general healing power, is needed to aid the situation and circumstances prevailing at that emergency site or area.

Where an individual is concerned, the personal progression of that soul is striving to grow and by initiating a personal inner examination from time to time, provides a fine-tuning and cleaning session to the shine of deliverance, which can benefit the individual in its clarity of vision, regarding the current people and circumstances presently contained within the material life. Your Guardian Angel is the first connection to the spiritual realms, and is so evenly attuned to your individual vibratory rate, that the connection may seem as if you are talking to your higher self.

It is your Guardian Angel who influences your consciousness to steer you clear, when you may be unguarded and openly vulnerable in your dealings. Remember to cloak yourself in golden light as a protective cloak and shield, and this will give you added strength at times when you feel unsteady. Know that your Guardian Angel will always respond when you make a conscious call for assistance. A flood of lighted essence will be forthcoming, and you will know you are truly blessed.

You may feel a tingling or a fluttering around you like a feather or butterfly that is so subtle that you hardly notice these feelings, but it is the response from your Guardian Angel who quivers in response to your communications and calls for assistance. For those who may not truly believe that the presence of their Guardian Angel is indeed a reality, they must test the connection by asking questions. If patience and quietness is adopted then the atmospheric changes can be felt and even the slight pressure of a hand upon a shoulder can be recognised. Sometimes a knowing of someone standing behind or at the side of you, can be recognised as the calling card of your Guardian Angel for each spirit entity can make themselves known by using an earthly sensation as their mode of recognition.

This applies to loved ones that have since passed into the spirit world, for how many times have you smelt the smoke of grand-fathers pipe or the perfume of mother's favourite scent or flower. Look for the white feathers you find when no bird is around. These are but some of the simple ways a Spirit or Angel can make their presence known to you. Be observant and be still, for you miss so much in the busy earthly world where your attention is continually working from dawn to dusk. Remember at the end of each day to send a prayer to your Guardian Guide for he or she is your greatest friend and will walk with you upon your life's pathway, and when it is the time to make your transition to the higher realms of existence, it will be your Guardian Angel who will hold your hand, and lead you to the eternal heavenly pastures, as you walk towards your new abode of light.

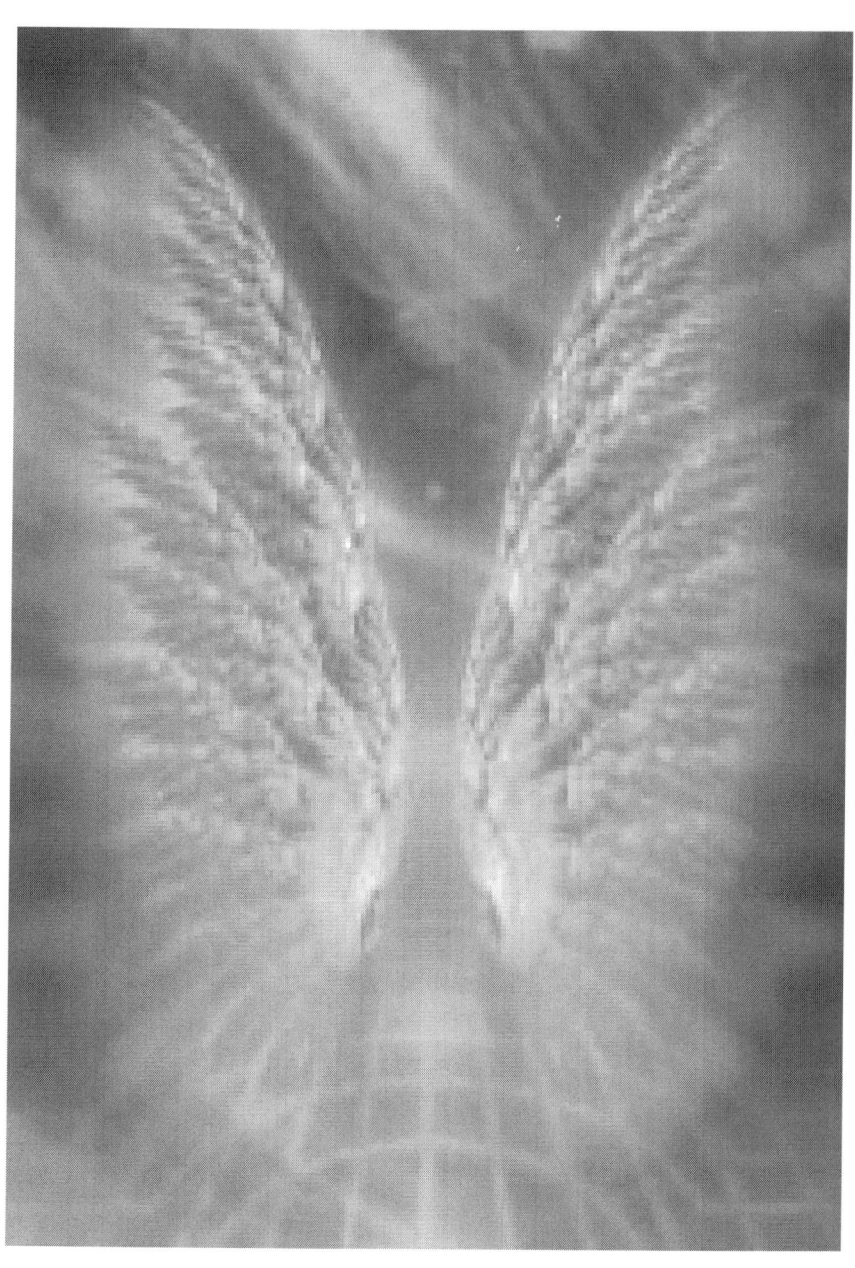

Angel Wings

Chapter 39

The Present

A true devotee is tested to the limits as their life is full of challenges both personal and professional. Many are able to overcome their hurdles within the professional life and it is an accomplishment to solve problems, particularly when viewed objectively and often impersonally. When someone shows exceptional talent in managing general affairs well, others are complimentary and offer praise. When however the problems manifest in the personal life, it is another matter.

The emotional vehicle of a human is ever vulnerable to discord and upheaval and when the balance of harmony is upset, the emotional storms can cause wide spread damage to the one in question. It is like steering a ship across the ocean. You may start out in the calm and then run into storms and tempests, and only the most stalwart will manage to steer correctly towards a scheduled destination. It may be that the emotional storm will divert and delay a human individual in its progressive course, because that self is not able out of fear, or not willing to take the risk on faith, to ride the storm. It is by becoming a crest upon a wave and seeing that the experience is a way to fast track progress, by using the nature of the currents, which are taking that individualized self, quickly forward. The individual self has to leave many things behind and the feelings associated with this shedding of things no longer relevant or desirable, can be painful and uncomfortable. If the individual shows aptitude for understanding the process of this great change, then pain and hurt can be minimised, as the focus is changed from the past to the present and then to the future.

Suffering depression is caused by looking at past events and situations. Anxiety is felt if the focus in upon the future which encompasses the unknown and produces fear for future events. This causes feelings of uncertainty to manifest as anxiousness. Endeavour to live in the present where there is peace and certainty, and do not worry about the past or the future, as the present is all you can influence. By doing so, the future will take care of itself, based upon the input of the present. The present time is one of great change in all departments of the living life. It brings many challenges to many people. It is how you deal with these challenges which is the important lesson of life, and the attitude you adopt when taking action, to sort situations out, to the best of your ability. This is a time where you will find out who your best friends are. They are the ones who come to your aide when all about you are turning their heads and hearts away. Those you thought of as friends may fall by the wayside, while others who you may have held with less importance, come forward to support and help.

What comes from experiencing emotional trauma is the awareness that many other individuals are lonely and depressed, because they also need help and consideration. They too are hurting in ways similar to you, and are desperately seeking solutions. While those in spirit can bring uplifting vibrations around a need, it is more effective when healing thoughts and actions are given from another earthly person, as the effects are immediate and are relayed on a sympathetic emotional level. When the mind comes to terms with the emotional swaying and can regulate any unwanted thoughts and feelings, the being becomes more balanced and can operate in a positive focus way, to deal with the material and physical aspects associated with the immediate problem. Physical energy expended in clearing up and clearing out unwanted baggage, will clear the place, air and atmosphere. This brings in new vibrations more settling to a harmonious atmosphere and will regenerate the person who had been suffering from the fall out of a negative explosion.

Once new positive energies are forthcoming the effects can be seen; the transformation of disposition as well as the realigning of the mindset, and also recharging of the physical energetic form. It is like a boat being beached and then refloated again. If the refloat is done straight away the boat will be as it was before, but if a little time is spend while beached and out of water, the renewal and repair of any damage or wear and tear can be put right. This enables the boat to be refloated as new. It shows a much better shape and appearance than before, so no one would associate the old worn and damaged boat with the renewed, repaired and repainted version now appearing in the present. The capabilities and attraction of this new vehicle attracts new interest, to allow it to acquire a new purpose and a new direction or pathway. The life processes gather momentum and the new pathway takes the vehicle into new uncharted waters for further life experiences. Such are the events of personal upheavals, change and renewals, for all energy in life has to change at some time, and it is best to accommodate these changes when they arise, and move with the tide into a more sheltered and safe harbour.

While the mind and intellect can move forward first, it is the emotions and physical vehicle of the body form which lags behind and sometimes takes time to catch up with the fastness of movement expected with sudden and demanding changes. Thoughts and emotions are often joined together and can become in conflict when the mind says one thing and the feelings are saying another. This is a time for meditating to distance the self and soul from the prevailing circumstances. When objectivity is obtained and can be achieved, the view of life events can be put into logical order and a more balanced perspective occurs. One step at a time is advocated when walking through the heavy material of emotional treacle. By being strong in determination with a focus on future positive happenings, an individual may overcome much of a turbulent nature and steer the human ship every closer to shore and safe harbour. When the cliffs of land can be seen there is hope and heartiness.

The energies rise again into a harmonious mix whereby the soul and self can actualise the present energies for beneficial outcomes. Creativity is employed anew, to bring a New Dawn of Enlightenment, a New Dawn of Achievement, a New Dawn of Beginnings, a New Dawn of Understanding. A new life unfolds, full of positive newness, love and fulfilment....so you can walk forward into your destiny to fulfil your life's purpose.

A World View

Chapter 40

The Light of the Soul

The soul is the counterpart of your physical body, and why it is not actually physical, conceptually it is as such, for it contains within it, all that you are. It is the soul light which guides you, and gravitates to other souls, with sympathetic vibrations that are likened to your own. The soul is like a bank of experience and knowledge. Your life experience in the dense physical world enables you to store knowledge and experience within the banks of wisdom. All things are stored energetically in the knowledge banks, and it is this evolution and growth, that enables the light of each soul to shine more brightly, as it progresses and grows to maturity.

You have often heard of old souls, and when an old soul decides to incarnate as a physical human being, it brings with it all the knowledge and wisdom built up over its existence and spiritual lifetimes, and that is why an old soul shines so brightly, even if it is contained within a young physical body. The knowledge and wisdom it holds brings guidance and instructions to others, to help them on the paths of progress to enlightenment, towards their own personal evolvement as a spiritual being or soul. And when a soul makes that transition back to the spirit realms and to its original homeland, it is often met but its own family of souls. These are family because they are complimentary, and often these complimentary souls form a group, as you are a present symbol. Groups form for many reasons.

It may be for a sympathetic project or it may be just to commune, one with another because they are linked energetically as in a family. And sometimes within a soul group you may well find that individual souls are incarnate at a time, when others may not be, and the life that is lived within the dense physical realm is often full of experiences, that are relayed to other members of the group, who are presently incarnate and to those who are not. For all members of the group absorb the knowledge of the one and of the many.

Sometimes a human being may become aware of a persona or a place which seems very familiar. You may jokingly say 'Oh I have been here before' or 'I know this person' when you have never met them before or have never been to that place before in this particular lifetime. Yet in your mind and in your knowledge you know. You know this person; you know this place for it is familiar because it resonates with your vibration and your note. It could well be that you have been here before, in another lifetime, in another memory, and the person who seems so familiar may indeed be one of your soul group. The permutations are wide and varied, for the purpose is often to provide a helping hand for the one who travels a difficult pathway.

The greater soul light, the greater shine that is always present, and this comes from the great source of creation. When it is recognised that each and everyone's own personal life is a fragment of the greater light, that shines for all and all things, then the knowledge that all is one and one is all, becomes an everlasting truth.

The attraction of vibrational light is always there, to draw you to truth, and often through the flame you may see with the inner eye, the truths you are seeking. Your focus is direct, and with the inner eye, you connect to the greater light of source. All souls are part of a great conglomerate, they are numerous as the stars in the sky, and they exist in a sea which is presently called upon the earth plane – humanity.

And all are at different levels with some bobbing along the surface, and some underneath the surface. But within the mix there is a variety and many colourful hues, for all are trying to connect in some way to the everlasting source, from within or without.

The attraction is for you to find, to draw to you the things and people of interest. Know that the glow from the flame, from the Great Source of Light, gives the love that is felt around and is presently encompassing all things. It may not always be visible, but it is always there.

I thank you all, for listening to my words

A Celestial Lightworker

Levitation

Chapter 41

The Future Times

When the present circumstances are accepted as being no longer necessary or beneficial it is time to change the thinking and practical living to something new and more positive. Time is of the essence to complete the changes relevant to bring in new energies, which will transform the physical life. It is when an individual takes control of the situation and determines to evoke the changes required, that the positive vibrations are forthcoming, to deliver the timely and purposeful formats, as incoming power that will transform as beneficial life circumstances of the near future and beyond.

In this time of great changes within the universe and the planet earth, which are affecting all creatures upon the surface, it is necessary to instil the ideas and values of the new age. It is selected Lightworkers that are forging ahead at great personal cost to themselves and their families. Individuals are experiencing a life that is turned upside down when familiar and existing relationships are severed abruptly, in favour of new and more creative connections. The quicker the transition from one state to another, the easer it is for the adaptation to new life circumstances to become the new reality. No longer will a sterile and unfulfilled life be experienced, but an excitement will prevail, of what will become the greatest fulfilment and joy of present living. With the New Age comes enlightenment of personal living and existence, to the many who have left former friends, partners and relations behind, who could not ascribed to the new ethics and new lifestyles of the Aquarian Age.

Those left behind will be given their reviews on entering into the spiritual heavens when their time is due, and they will see that the decision to stay the same and be unmovable was a decision that they will have to redress in the due course of eternal existence. Those who have recognised the lightworkers way and gravitated to like minded hearts and minds, they will see the fulfilment of their decisions in the beneficial changes brought about within their own lives, their own locality and their own country.

The future will look bright to all lighted persons who embrace the New Age fully, as all possible lighted wavelengths will converge upon the knowing, who can utilise and transpose energy formats into useful manifestations, to become part of the environments newness and future times. Look forward to the exciting times that will come your way, personally and collectively, as the earth life changes take place. As a pack of cards fall, so too will the changes revolutionise the living life, so all may become witness to the worlds of lighter vibrations becoming one with the earth plane. This will occur when the present dense energy of the earth planet is transformed into a lighter format, so it may blend with the present overlaying etheric vibrations.

The human senses will become enhanced so that the super-senses of clairvoyance, clairaudience and clairsentience will be normal modes of operation for most humans. This will be as a result of revitalised DNA strands, which will come into the next generation of human beings. The children will lead many adults who do not have the faculty of awareness as a natural gift and talent. Those adults who have trained their ability of awareness by developing their super-senses will have the advantage, for they will be the forward vanguard of the race.

It is they who are the stalwarts of your present society, and are the ones to follow, for it is they who shine their lighted presence for all to see. The lightworkers are gathering force as the cohesion intensifies. Many are forming brotherhoods and sisterhoods as like attracts like. Soon the groups and organisations of lightworkers will dominate every aspect of living, and then the world of earthly men and women will become as one. Wars will end as they serve no purpose. Co-operation will reign and the distribution of food, medical supplies and wealth with be more evenly spread. There will be much rebuilding after disasters have taken their toll, which will be brought about by the eradication of much negativity. New growth and new ways will be forthcoming, and humans everywhere will welcome a collective fresh approach.

Know that the present age is the beginning of something great, which can only come into being by a radical change within the living life. Once this is understood and accepted as a premise, then the work of forward manifestation can commence in earnest. The New Dawn will herald in a New Age of Understanding and Co-operation. The New Dawn of your future time will bring great enlightenment. The health and welfare of all humans will improve substantially. Love and Brotherhood will become a normal aspiration and put into action will change all that is within the world of earthlings.

Know that as you walk your forward path, the light of source is always ahead illuminating your way. Follow that light, follow your hearts calling and you will walk the paths of truth and shine your own light for many to see. Become the God of your own creation as you adopt a life of harmlessness, kindness and caring. Pray to your spirit friends who offer help and assistance and are only but a thought away. In doing so you evoke heavenly assistance and can by collective thoughts manifest the desired changes necessary for the illumination of the New Dawn of your New Day. Bless all who follow the wisdom words, Bless all who put such thoughts into action.

May goodness and purity be your values to allow the human light to merge with the celestial light, and so bring the all, into the one perfected whole.

Open Your Heart

Chapter 42

Be who you really are.

When a child be as a child, but when you become an adult, put away childish things and mature into the soul you really are.

The emergence of the matured self is like the flowering of a plant or the emergence of a butterfly. It is a real transformation, of the being, from one state to another. Rarely do humans see this process or recognise it for what it is. It does however occur when tragedy or misfortune has occurred, to upset the present life and transform the physical circumstances into something entirely different. One minute a human being may be an ordinary person doing ordinary things, and the next minute he or she is thrust into the limelight, and may be known globally for some deed or accomplishment, that up to now has seemed unimportant and insignificant.

Suddenly however the universe has manoeuvred the energies into action, to bring about a transformation, so that a specific human may shine a gift or talent, amongst a wide environment or world scene. It seems that this person has been lifted up above ordinary folk, as someone important, and it is very significant to other folk that the masses should take note. At such times of greatness when thrust upon the shoulders of an unsuspecting human, it takes a little time to digest and absorb. Once acceptance is forthcoming the greatness is only seen by observers, for the one who has been singled out to be honoured, is often unaware of how they have impacted upon the many. They only know their life has flowered beyond comparison of what has gone before.

The hurt and pain of previous times is forgotten in the wake of such brightness and glory, being bestowed upon the personality of the one who is being singled out as special.

The Dawn of the New Age of awareness will bring many changes which will transform the lives of many individuals. Much will be left behind of old ties and cleavages which had once seemed so strong and necessary. However the new energies will bring compensations within the physical life, which will become the new glory and brilliance of modern day living. Lives will be transformed in ways not imagined. Think of the coming times as a wonderful journey into lighted realms, where you as an individual, may shine your inner light and actualized the 'I am presence' of your own true being. Your soul and spirit will shine through for others to see and recognise, so you will become secure within your energetic light brilliance, and merge only with those of equal shine.

Those relationships you attract to you will be of equal or compensating measure. It will be a case of the two becoming as one energetically, as the two will make a greater whole. Soul groups will join together to make Ashrams of note. All group souls will become a towering apex of communicating channels between the varying dimensions. You will find an interesting mix of peoples coming together in each group, as the spectrum of operative ability, will stretch from the elemental to the celestial.

It is the merging of the dimensional levels that the most interesting life forms will emerge. Physical and near etheric will become as one with many individuals able to see and communicate with semi-physical entities. These will include loved ones who have passed from the physical realm, who wish to stay close by, to help their relatives and perhaps wait for them until their time upon the physical plane is ended. In addition the elementals of earth, fire, water and air will begin to become recognised and in some cases, work with enlightened humans in ways that are beneficial for the planet and human living.

Chapter 43

Love is in the Air.

As L.O.V.E. is the light of vital energy for all earth existence and being, then the saying of Love is in the Air is a truism. The very essence of life giving energy and vibrations are carried in and through the air waves and currents, to bring to all living things upon the earth world, that vital energy from which to grow and become. The air permeates many denser substances even earth and water, and fire needs air in order to burn, otherwise it becomes extinguished. Often more than two elements bind together to bring shape and substance to forms, and always the air is around to provide a media of transference. Like the waterways the air also has currents, which can flow fast or slow, hot or cold, fierce or weak, gently or harsh. A gentle breeze sooths many a fractured brow whereas a strong fierce storm can fuel the human emotions into a cyclone of rage. A cool or cold wind is welcomed in a hot climate and likewise a warm or hot wind is appreciated at times of coldness.

Vegetation grows with the help of earth, water and air. It assists a plant that may flower and bloom when exposed into the air environment, where the sunlight can access the earth's surface to encourage newness and form into growing. The air defuses the strong sunlight to bring acceptable levels to the many flowers and fauna, which cover the earth's surface. It can act as a filter and may be more heavily concentrated with oxygen at lower levels, than at high elevations. Vegetation adapts to prevailing energy and nutriments to show itself in varying form and sizes.

When the saying of 'Love is in the Air' becomes meaningful it is when human emotions are heightened to register the impact of feeling the love vibrations, which translates as human emotion becoming tangibly felt. It is an uplifting feeling, bringing a sense of well being and comfort. Universal love is the general healing power transmitted through the airways so that all peoples everywhere can breathe it into their human bodyform, and energise themselves, by using the breath and absorbing the nutriments contained therein, for the body and minds affective functioning. Love is in the Air is a truism, believe it and know it, as from the air your life is filled with new vitality and wisdom as these qualities are carried on the in-breath of life itself.

Those who practice such methods such as in Buddhist meditations based on the breath, know full well the importance and benefits of breath, and the breathing in of the Prana or life energy within the substance of air. There are even organisations which promote the correct methods of breathing the air, to enhance body performance whether that is to assist a malfunction or damaged part to right itself, or to enhance physical excellence for sport or entertainment purposes. For those who can undertake deep breathing exercises, the benefits become tangible assets in physical performance. Others can develop limited breathing for underwater activities, where holding the breath is necessary for long periods. Natives who dive for pearls can hold their breath for what seems to be a long time, compared to normal breathing rates and activity of others not engaged in such pursuits.

When 'Love is in the Air' there are electrical currents surging through the Airwaves and this is felt or sensed by those humans who are connected to such currents. Thoughts are carried upon the Airwaves and as a result, help and healing is sent to recipients as requested and sent by others, or needed by the one who has asked. Present day airwaves are saturated by radio waves, sound and colour waves, Ultra-Violet and Infer-Red are other energy waves of importance.

Gamma and Cosmic waves come from outer space and are infiltrating within the airwaves in a stepped down mode, which does not devastate or harm in any way. All is carried upon the air, in currents and flows, of varying strength and cordiality. The air is definitely full of life providing elements, as demonstrated by the amount of continual growth and renewal shown in evolving occurrences. In changing climates, and in different terrains, the air takes charge of vegetative growth and determines the extent of blooms and harvest. In cold and warm weather conditions, the airways carry vital elements for the nourishment of living forms.

Without life within the airways the atmosphere would become a vacuum which would leave all life in an inert condition. Static life showing its form in suspension, framed for eternity in a still and unmoving environment. The air is not static but a moving and flowing media for goodness, where nourishment is transported to recipient sites where growth movement ensues. It is the breadth of God, for that which humans call God is the omnipresent power and force of source life. The eternal creator and creative power brings to all manifested life, the form, vitality and animation of moving parts. Movement is progress in action. Action is the result of the though-mind process which continually flow ideas and thoughts into animated brains.

Humans are not the only large brain animals inhabiting the earth plane. You know this because of the interaction of the large whales and dolphins of your oceans with those of your scientist who have devoted their life and time to studding such creatures. Humans are the chosen creatures who were given dominion over all others upon the earth planet. The responsibility for animal life and welfare rests with humans for they have reasoning power. The love given to individual animals can be seen in their response to their human masters. Humanising animals brings the animal souls into individualisation and this arrives through the given love animating from the human heart. Such is the love that is passed through the Air.

Cosmic Man

Chapter 44

Changing Your Note

I attended my local church on their evening of Healing where they conducted a healing service involving the laying on of hands. This was something I had been doing weekly for the past 4 years as my way of receiving beneficial energy for my physical body which had suffered cancer in 2008. I had elected to receive spiritual healing instead of conventional treatment of radiotherapy, and had received weekly healing as a way of keeping up my good health and vitality for all my life activities.

On his particular occasion I had brought a friend to this Healing service, who also required healing after her recent operation. The moment I sat on the chair and closed my eyes, I was transported into another dimension. I had become aware of my Nun Guide who is always present when healing is taking place, and also when I engage in other activities when working with spirit. Sister Maria took me into a church and laid me on a healing bed which was placed half way down the aisle in the middle of this large old church. My head was facing the altar and I was aware of a fine golden cross with golden goblets place upon the altar as if ready for a service.

Sister Maria was accompanied by a number of other nuns all dressed in white, who came to stand shoulder to shoulder around the healing bed on which I was lying. Their presence became a wall surrounding my being, so shutting out the presence of large light beings or angels, who were standing behind this wall of healing nuns.

I instinctively knew that the healing angels were the source of the healing energies which would be passed down to the healing nuns and then passed through their ministrations to my auric field which I could see manifesting as a dome around me. There was a moment of stillness or hesitation before the command of ignition, as the angels of light, literally - lit up. It was like a switch being switched on and activated, so light was generated and shone brightly. I knew and felt the beginning of an electrified energy as this light seeped between the cracks separating each of the healing nuns. I had been plugged in. I knew at that moment that the healing angels were the first source of healing energy and that they were sending their light to the healing nuns who would then pass the appropriate amount to me. A three tiered structure or three level light passage of healing energy.

The healing nuns lit up also and flooded me with their light by placing their hands upon my auric dome. I felt like a newly lit light bulb, one of those modern ones which gather brilliance the longer it's left on. Just as I felt as if I would burst, the pressure was released when the nun at my head stepped back. Then the nun at my feet also stepped back. A golden line of light flooded my aura from north to south. I became aware that at each side of me which was east and west, the nuns had also stood back and another line of golden light crossed over my heart from one arm to the other. The two lines of golden light formed a cross and when this dawned upon my consciousness, I felt the love emotion flood my whole being. I knew that these two lines of light represented the Christ energies of love and healing, and that somehow it felt right that I should be receiving these energies. This resonated with my knowledge of my connection to the Christian family. I felt whole, I felt complete, I felt reborn.

I became aware that other healing nuns were stepping back and forth within the circle they had formed around me. This caused a rhythm to form and altered my ringtone.

The analogy of a piano formed in my mind as the movement of the healing nuns created a tempo of music, just like a piano key activates a hammer to ring a note, so too were these healing nuns moving in and out, to bring about a tune which resonated a change of note within me. I realised there was a purpose for this action, as my energetic being was being changed to coincide to the new note of the New Dawn of the New Age. I also realised that this type of healing activity was not only for me, but was taking place each time earthly healing was given, so as to align the human energy note to that of the 2012 Ascension.

By changing human ringtones to the new dimensional energy waves, the human individual and groups would be carried along upon the crest of new dimensional incoming waves. This will enable the new energy patterns to be absorbed within the human aura, so that the mind can be activated, and leap to higher levels, within the multidimensional planes of existence. When the healing had finished the healing nuns all stood back to allow me space. I was all alight and glowing. I felt vitalised and on top of the world. I saw myself encased within my aura of scintillating light, which was having a wonderful effect upon me. My mind had been cleared of depressive thoughts as all was bright and positive. My emotions were balanced as I felt calm and serene. My spirit was back with renewed brightness, and I knew that any physical distress I was feeling was just the residue of negativity flowing out of my body.

This state of being was something of a surprise, as on the material plane and in the physical life, I faced many problems arising from recent deaths and partings, which a moment ago had seemed insurmountable. Now I had no fear. I was confident that all my problems were just irritations, and that my focus was on my spiritual pursuits, which were far more important, as the expectations and needs of the many, outweighed the needs of the one or few.

In a few short months since the death of my father, my life had been cleared of debris and negativity. When this happens, the universe is saying that something new and better is coming into the physical life. These times of Ascension may not be easy for everyone, but if your note is called, you must respond, for your destiny lies within new bands of activity, which will include new people to fill your life needs.

Allow the New Dawn into your life, as the New Age reveals its hidden pleasures and joy. Keep the faith of your understanding to know that God loves all his children who are unique and beautiful in his eyes. Blessings will surely follow you, as you reach up into the arms of the one who loves you most.

Nameste

End Note

Alluisha, **12.12.12**

Greetings from the celestial sources, for you evoke the Angels of the Heavens to you by your calls of light at this time. We surround you and your world, as you open to the celestial powers of light to soak your planet in beautiful and cleansing vibrations, which are much lighter and finer, so your dense energy fields are made weaker. This allows more light to enter into the etheric fields surrounding your physical forms. Pastel colours can merge and transform into other hues, far easier than stronger prime colours, which make up a definite statement. The new energies of your planet and all that exist upon it are becoming increasingly more lighter in hue and texture.

The crystaline deposits of your earth material have been charged once again with active ingredients, so they will discharge their power into your world with a most edifying effect. Your energy centres or chakras are receiving new resonations with the effect of lifting the emotions a peg or two, so you may feel greater responses, and become aware of other peoples responses as well as your own. This is the empathy effect that may cause some folk to make adjustments to their way of being, as the changes within will need balancing for best working and comfort. Like all your mechanical vehicles which require servicing and tune-ups, there is a time for running in, so that the newly cleaned apparatus can function more effectively and more productively.

Know at this time the heavens open to allow the pouring of divine light into your central sun, which is you life giver. Your planet is special and is now a sacred shrine for many other planets, whose evolution can benefit from the lessons learned from human beings.

The playground of experiences is a fast learning place for soul evolution and provides the means of fast tracking many who seek to enter into the higher realms of existence. The earth journey is not taken lightly, for all souls choose to incarnate in a life they themselves have chosen to undertake.

When entering into the earth realm the previous inherited life is forgotten or hidden, so as not to influence the living personality who will judge, value and condone things it does not understand fully because it has not been proved. In the years ahead, new human beings will remember their previous heritage and as a result of greater knowledge from previous lives, will bring forth greater and more meaningful concepts for the race to adopt, so better life and living conditions can be established as well as ensuing relationships.

The New Age of enlightenment will indeed seem revolutionary to what you know from the now. The psychic sciences will be a normal mode of operation for many, and many will be respected for their individual abilities. ESP will become widespread, Telepathy, Psychometry and Remote Viewing or Out of the Body experiences, will be common place. All these things will evolve from the greater love capacity that will flow from the newly awakened centres of the human heart and minds, which have fully become activated.

It is the Love aspect of divine power which changes everything and can manifest anything charged with Divine Will. Connect to your central sun source and know that you and your God are one. Demonstrate the divine essence of love by giving your hand in friendship and helping others less able than yourself. Become a healing agent for divine light and love, and know as you offer that healing it will take place. It has to, because of universal law which governs the light power of positive vibrations says 'As you think so it becomes'. The power is within you. The light is within you. God is within you.

You are your own creative power, so use your gifts wisely and for the greatest benefit or for the highest good. God is wise and so are you, if you can use your quiet space within to listen to your divine guidance. God always steers you in the best way for you. Never doubt the higher power of the God source. It will never let you down, for the well of energy light is never ending, and as your needs arise, so God's essence is given freely and selflessly to fill your needs. Gods work continues so his children may live in the paradise of his vision. Be joyful, Be loving, Be blessed.

...... 0 ......

The year of 2013 begins for it is a year of six. The feminine aspect of all things will assert itself and the power of nine being the masculine, will attempt to challenge each step of the way. The light female energy will balance and harmonize, and will chase the denseness away, for light always subdues the darker hues. By demonstrating positive thoughts and will power, you evoke the positive energy around you. The unseen elementals respond to positive though power and you will find you have many hidden helpers to assist you in your endeavours. Enjoy the life you have chosen for it is your pathway to greater things.

Blessing to all…….. Alluisha, Alluisha.

The End